THE MODERN SCHOOL SUPERINTENDENT

THE MODERN SCHOOL SUPERINTENDENT

◆

An Overview of the Role and Responsibilities in the 21st Century

Marvin E. Edwards

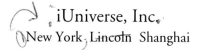

iUniverse, Inc.
New York Lincoln Shanghai

THE MODERN SCHOOL SUPERINTENDENT
An Overview of the Role and Responsibilities in the 21st Century

Copyright © 2006, 2007 by Marvin E. Edwards

All rights reserved. No part of this book may be used or reproduced by any means, graphic, electronic, or mechanical, including photocopying, recording, taping or by any information storage retrieval system without the written permission of the publisher except in the case of brief quotations embodied in critical articles and reviews.

iUniverse books may be ordered through booksellers or by contacting:

iUniverse
2021 Pine Lake Road, Suite 100
Lincoln, NE 68512
www.iuniverse.com
1-800-Authors (1-800-288-4677)

The views expressed in this work are solely those of the author and do not necessarily reflect the views of the publisher, and the publisher hereby disclaims any responsibility for them.

ISBN-13: 978-0-595-40874-0 (pbk)
ISBN-13: 978-0-595-85392-2 (cloth)
ISBN-13: 978-0-595-85238-3 (ebk)
ISBN-10: 0-595-40874-5 (pbk)
ISBN-10: 0-595-85392-7 (cloth)
ISBN-10: 0-595-85238-6 (ebk)

Printed in the United States of America

Contents

Preface ix
Introduction xi

Part I Becoming a School Superintendent

Chapter 1 The Evolution of the School Superintendency 3
Chapter 2 Paths to the Superintendency 14
Chapter 3 Laying the Groundwork for Success 25

Part II Mastery of the Profession

Chapter 4 Superintendent–School Board Relations 41
Chapter 5 Internal and External Relations 57
Chapter 6 Government Relations 71
Chapter 7 Fiscal Responsibility 82
Chapter 8 Managing Conflicts and Crises 97
Chapter 9 The Dynamics of Leadership and Change 114
Chapter 10 Political Savvy and the Superintendency 128

Part III Meet Eight Superintendents

Chapter 11 Arcadia: Opening Communication Channels 141
Chapter 12 Barnet: Risky Politics 149

Chapter 13	Cambay: Harsh Fiscal Realities	157
Chapter 14	Darwin: The Storm of Social Change	168
Chapter 15	Epirus: A Balancing Act	179
Chapter 16	Finley: Mediawise Superintendent	189
Chapter 17	Gambia: Urban Reform	198
Chapter 18	Harrow: A Turnaround Challenge	211

Part IV CONCLUSION

The Superintendent of the Future 221

References 236

About the Author 247

Acknowledgements

A special thanks to all of my colleagues and mentors from across the years that made the completion of this work possible. There is no need to list those who provided influence and support since they will recognize their contributions throughout the pages of this book. Special mention is due colleagues, Larry Ascough and Ronald O'Neal who read, critiqued and edited early drafts of the manuscript.

While many people made this book possible both directly and indirectly, it was because of my family that the will to complete the work was uncompromising. My loving wife, Carolyn and our five adult children along with their spouses and our grandchildren were the catalyst for me to not allow failure as an option. I pray that all of their lives will be influenced by this book in such a way that they too will value the power of never giving up on a dream.

Preface

Today's superintendents—and those who expect to serve in the schools of the future—must deal with situations that are considerably more complex than those faced by their predecessors. While the job of superintendent has never been considered easy, growing expectations have made it far more difficult to successfully maintain the position without adequately comprehending the issues and frustrations involved, as well as the necessary responses and remedies that are required.

The job of a school superintendent in America is vastly misunderstood by the masses. As a practitioner and scholar, the author knows firsthand that many institutions and individuals lack real understanding when it comes to the superintendency. That conclusion is based on the author's 35 years as a public school educator in four states—including 23 years as a superintendent of schools—and his association with numerous superintendents. Yet in examining the literature, it is evident that there is a dearth of information written specifically about the modern superintendency. While there is an abundance of material on the subject of leadership and its various facets, the superintendency itself appears not to have been widely researched. Studying leadership in other venues can be instructive and transferable to the superintendency in some cases, but the superintendency is a unique enterprise that requires specialized leadership skills.

Influenced by observing the work and behavior of superintendent colleagues, this book is intended to provide the reader with a base of knowledge regarding the pressures related to the position of the superintendent and the evolving expectations that are inherent in serving in this vital role. The goal is to help the reader come to know what it is really like to be a superintendent in today's challenging environment, increase awareness of the enormous responsibility and the difficulties associated with the role, and create a realization of how successful leadership as a superintendent is linked to the future of American education.

It is time that the superintendency is given the proper attention it deserves.

Introduction

An impossible job? That's what many have called the superintendency. With its growing and competing demands, it is a profession that can baffle even the most knowledgeable and well prepared. Public education resources have become more limited. There are new national and state testing requirements. Social issues are being pulled into our school systems. Communities are losing faith in public schools and want more control over their operation. Add in politics and bureaucracy, and the end result is quite an unmanageable scenario.

Yet the office it is not all doom and gloom. Offering opportunities that are unavailable in many other careers, the superintendency is a position in which you will be taken seriously by others. And it is a profession in which one person, through skilled leadership, can make a difference by getting everyone to pull together and create a better learning environment for students. Surveys actually have shown that most superintendents would become a superintendent again if they had the chance.

Unfortunately, more superintendents seem to be leaving the profession, and some question both the drop in the number of applicants and their qualifications. Whether it is because of the current demands superintendents face, the quality of preparation and professional development programs, or a combination of both, the trend is a growing concern. Many superintendents are clearly unprepared to deal with what they may encounter in running a school district. Part of that problem has been blamed on the weak link between theory and application in superintendent preparation programs. Another major issue has been unrealistic job expectations, or assuming more can be accomplished by one superintendent than is actually possible.

That's where this book can help: It presents an overview of what the job of a superintendent really entails on a daily basis, taking a look at what works and what doesn't when you're a practicing superintendent out in the field. While much of the information contained in this book is based on the actual experiences of superintendents—both the author's and those whom the author has met—it applies formal training to realistic examples of situations superintendents face on the job every day. The characteristics and insights of successful superintendents are described, along with some of the strategies they use.

Any reader who wants to understand the intricacies of the American school superintendency should find this book helpful. Current practicing school superintendents can use the scenarios described herein to compare, contrast, or verify their own experiences, as it is intended that the approaches to leadership discussed may be instructive to those who are seeking guidance.

Another important audience for this information is school board members who are either currently on a school board or are considering the job. Clearly a discussion of the superintendency cannot be separated from the presence and significance of the board. The workings of a good school board are often enhanced by the employment of a capable superintendent. Therefore, school board members should find this book very relevant to their work with the superintendent.

Central office administrators and principals who may intend to become school superintendents in the future, or may simply want to more fully understand the big picture of the superintendency to enhance their own efforts, should benefit from this book. Whichever is the case, the better understanding that staff members have of the superintendency, the better the entire organization.

This book can also serve as a resource for graduate study. Students who have the goal of assuming the role of superintendent at the completion of their study should find this book useful. Such students will have typically served in high levels of school administration and are concentrating on scholarly study to prepare them for the transition to the superintendency.

Finally, there are teachers, and others curious about the superintendency, who may be seeking a source for learning. This book will provide a basic understanding for anyone in education, or even someone with a general interest, who is looking for a reliable source of information about the superintendency.

You will find this book is divided into four parts:

Part I—Becoming a School Superintendent
> This section contains chapters 1 through 3. Starting from the evolution of the superintendency, through preparation, training, and on to the first duties required of a new superintendent, these chapters are foundational and prepare the reader to better comprehend and appreciate the information that follows.

Part II—Mastery of the Profession
> Chapters 4 through 10 move beyond the basics. These chapters cover more specific topics, such as working with the school board and government relations. They will help the reader to more fully understand what the modern superintendency as a profession is all about.

Part III—Meet Eight School Superintendents
> This section contains realistic profiles that illustrate the complex issues facing superintendents today. You will be introduced to eight different superintendents in school districts located in the midwestern, southeastern, and southwestern regions of the United States. These districts actually exist, and the superintendents described are the actual people who occupied the positions during the time period discussed. While the people are real, the names of the districts and the superintendents, as well as the details, have been altered enough to ensure anonymity.

Part IV—Conclusion
> This final chapter reexamines some of the points presented earlier. However it takes the discussion a step further, considering the implications for the school superintendency in the coming years in light of the profession's current status and the evolving demands on superintendents.

As writers of previous works have indicated, the superintendency is a dynamic position—always changing, and bringing with it challenges that vary as much as the school districts.

The experiences of the superintendents observed, and that of the author, highlight the fact that school district leadership is shaped by overlapping contexts, and ever present historical, national, and local issues. To be effective and enhance their chances for success, superintendents must know how to continually adjust their actions to meet the multilayered and competing demands of diverse interests. And while this book may reflect the author's own experiences as a superintendent, along with observations of other superintendents, that experiential viewpoint should not be discounted. For it is the practical involvement in day-to-day school district operations that defines the perspective of each superintendent and adds to the growing knowledge base of the profession.

PART I

Becoming a School Superintendent

1
The Evolution of the School Superintendency

In order to have a clear understanding of the superintendency as discussed in this book, it is necessary to provide some historical background as to how the position of the school superintendent evolved. When the term *superintendent of schools* is used, some might conclude that it refers to the state superintendency. Except for the brief reference in this chapter, this book pertains to local district superintendents and not superintendents at the state level.

The evolution of the superintendent's position parallels the progression of schools from a single room to multiform schools (Brubacher, 1966), to multibuilding school districts. The first state superintendency was established in 1812 in New York. Between 1830 and 1850, every northern state and some southern states created an office of state superintendent. By 1880, 24 states had set up their own state boards of education. The duties of the state superintendent included forming a plan for a common school system, reporting how public funds were being managed, and providing the state legislature with school-related information (Butts & Cremin, 1953). School districts were created by the states as the organizational units of government to administer the state's public education system (Hoyle, et al., 2005). The state agencies would oversee public education while delegating select policy powers to local school boards, effectively making local boards legal extensions of state government. This setup was to ensure that students in each state would be taught a fairly uniform curriculum and receive a similar educational experience (Kowalski, 1999).

The state superintendent is indeed the chief state officer authorized by the legislature with oversight and regulatory responsibility for all school districts within a state. Yet the state superintendent has little or no authority over the day-to-day function of local school districts. Those who hold the position of state superintendent, sometimes called commissioner of education, are often considered the educational leaders charged with and dedicated to fighting forces which may appear to hinder the development of the state's school system. However it is the legislature that legally represents the state in its responsibility for schools. Depending upon the state, a state board of education or the governor appoints the state superintendent, and in some cases the voters elect the state superintendent. At best, a state superintendent serves education by acting as an advocate for local school districts while functioning as an agent of the state. There is no illusion that a state superintendent is a supervisor of local school district superintendents, and it is clear that the role is important in relation to the fact that public education by law is a function of the state. An effective chief state school official is one who performs his or her duties as the state's intermediary and at the same time usually enjoys the respect of local school district officials while acting as an advocate for local educational issues.

Frequently in the early development of public education it was common for one teacher to be in charge of a school. Later, the in-charge teacher was referred to as a *head teacher*. As the development of schools progressed, the head teacher became known as the principal teacher, with certain authority over the other teachers. Schools grew even larger and operations became more complex. The principal teacher became the full-time building principal in many schools. Eventually, schools began to appoint full-time building principals as a standard. Thus, the principalship emerged in American education long before the superintendency.

In the early days of the public education system, a committee made up of laymen or townspeople, primarily community members, was appointed to handle the task of education administration (Owen & Ovando, 2000). In

1642, The Massachusetts School Ordinance was passed, further recognizing the necessity of school-specific management. According to the ordinance, every town would choose a group of men to manage all that was connected to schooling. They would determine local taxes, hire teachers, set wages, and decide on the length of the school year (Campbell, et al., 1990). In essence, these men who were to oversee the schools would later become known as the school board.

Villages or communities grew into cities and towns. Several school buildings formed a school district, and the supervision of schools by school committee became unworkable. The need arose for systemwide administration and supervision. The concept of a school committee found its way to other states, but members of these boards realized they could no longer handle all the day-to-day duties associated with running the schools. With district size growing, especially in more densely populated areas, so did the responsibilities. They would require a person apart from the board to handle the district's administrative functions (Sharp & Walter, 2004). The school leaders, however, were not interested in putting their faith in a single person until other methods of oversight were no longer effective, and even then not without a struggle (Owen & Ovando, 2000). But a single overseer finally did replace the committee. The first local school superintendent was appointed in June 1837 in Buffalo, New York (Carter & Cunningham, 1997; Sharp & Walter, 2004). At that time, the person who was hired and designated as the superintendent was also a layman (Owen & Ovando, 2000), basically cut from the same cloth as the committee. The difference was that the superintendency became a full-time job, thus providing the proper time to supervise and inspect the schools. This person was often paid less than the principal, who was the professional educator in the system.

It was during the common school movement—from 1830 to 1850—and the quest to build a system of state public elementary and secondary schools that the superintendency emerged (Kowalski, 1999). So even in those early years, many superintendents faced serious challenges, including the survival of the common school movement itself. They took on the job as true education reformers, spreading the word about a free public education from cities to villages (Glass, 2000c). The first superintendents were appointed in large cities, since local boards could still handle supervisory duties in smaller schools.

But as those small schools combined into districts, more boards began to appoint superintendents (Sharp & Walter, 2004). Between 1837 and 1850, 13 urban school districts created a position called the superintendency (Kowalski, 1999). During the next century, the growth of the superintendency closely followed the growth of public schools. By 1860, 27 cities with school districts had superintendents (Callahan, 1966). By 1880, 34 of the 38 United States had made provisions for the position. And as of 1890, all large U.S. cities had school superintendents, but they were not found in small towns until well into the 20th century (Carter & Cunningham, 1997).

Early 20th century superintendents were almost exclusively men (Glass, 1997), since women in those days were expected to stay in the classroom. As a matter of fact, the female teachers also were always single; married women were not allowed to teach in American public schools during that era. Many of the early superintendents, especially in rural America, traveled between several schools or districts. These pioneers were the overseers of the schools in the tradition of a circuit rider.

Not only were women not seen in the superintendent's role in the early days, members of ethnic minority groups also did not hold superintendencies. Although there are undocumented reports of blacks serving as superintendents before the late 1950s, there was no mention of their existence in records or literature in the education profession. A 1973 survey conducted by the National Alliance of Black School Educators did account for three black superintendents as early as 1956 in Oklahoma, Illinois, and Missouri. At the time of the survey, there were approximately 16,700 superintendents in the nation, of which 44 were black. Women held 86 of those positions, and there is no record of Hispanic superintendents during that period (Scott, 1980).

The school superintendent has had many different roles throughout history, often overlapping. The original role was that of a schoolmaster—a head teacher and clerk—with a lay school committee making most important decisions (Carter & Cunningham, 1997). The school boards interacted directly with school employees such as teachers and principals (Glass, 2000d). From the mid-1800s to about 1910, superintendents spent much of their energy on duties that would include maintaining orderly schoolhouses, supervising teachers, and implementing curricula (Carter & Cunningham, 1997; Kowalski, 1999). By the end of the 19th century, most superintendents were thought of as master teachers and educators (Carter and Cunningham, 1997) and were given duties other than secretarial and instructional (Owen & Ovando, 2000). As the importance of the superintendency became increasingly apparent, the responsibilities of the office were gradually expanded to include day-to-day district administration, as opposed to mere oversight.

From 1910 to 1930, superintendents focused on managing resources and establishing themselves as business managers (Callahan, 1966). Gradually after 1920, they also became viewed as democratic leaders or statesman, broadening their participation in educational decisions and managing the political environment created by that participation (Kowalski, 1999). From the 1920s, both superintendents and principals were recognized as educational "experts" of local school districts and were seldom challenged until the 1960s (Glass, 1997), when many parents and board members believed schools were not meeting community expectations (Spring, 1998).

From the mid-1950s to the mid-1960s, the superintendent as democratic leader was replaced by the superintendent as a combined educational realist and applied social scientist (Callahan, 1966), until reformers of the 1960s and 1970s questioned scientific management models of the urban school organization (Glass, 1997). In the 1960s and 1970s, demands from the public and pressure from interest groups forced superintendents to expand their roles in political leadership at both community and state levels (Hoyle, et al., 2005). And the primary view of superintendents from the 1960s until today is that of chief executive officers of the board, where they serve as a professional advisor, reform leader, resource manager, and public communicator (Carter & Cunningham, 1997).

Most men who were appointed superintendent in the formative years of the profession, especially during the 19th century, were teachers who had no training in managing people, finances, or other material resources (Kowalski, 1999). But with the growth in the office's responsibilities, the qualifications for the position became more professional. Prior to the turn of the 20th century, school systems grew larger and administration more complicated, and the educational administration profession evolved (Chapman, 1997).

School administrators actually began to organize as a profession separate from teachers as soon as the 1890s (Glasman & Fuller, 2002). Staff was added to assist the superintendent in specific areas, such as curriculum, business management, and personnel administration, as well as with buildings and grounds. Greatly concerned with the professional preparation of future administrators, some of the pioneering superintendents went into university teaching and founded departments of educational administration (Glass, 1997). After the turn of the century, the study of educational administration and supervision was introduced into the curriculum of graduate schools of education across the country.

From about 1900 to 1920, professors of education increased the course offerings in administration, especially in business management, finance, and efficiency techniques (Kowalski, 1999). Certification requirements for administrative positions were established by state legislatures. The superintendency became a position in and of itself, instituted by law in various states, and with its own unique certification requirements. The working relationship and lines of authority between school boards and superintendents evolved over the last 100 years in several stages. Before 1900, superintendents were pretty much general supervisors and board members set policy and made decisions.

After the turn of the century, many superintendents became business ideology advocates, stating that superintendents should be highly-trained professionals (Callahan, 1966). By the late 1920s, most states had outlined the legal responsibilities of both the school board and the superintendent in statutes, clarifying their authority and holding the superintendent responsible to the local board (Glass, 2000c), which set the current organizational form for today's school districts (Glass, 1997).

Under most state legal definitions, the superintendent of schools is regarded as the chief executive officer of the lay school board and the educational leader of the school district. Even though the legal status of the superintendent's employment provisions is not well-defined in some states, the position of school superintendent for all local school districts comes under state oversight. In most states, the superintendent has no legal, continued contractual right as is accorded teachers. The standard model is that the superintendent usually serves a short-term contract of two to five years, with the option to renew or extend it at the discretion of the local school board.

The importance of the position of school superintendent has been well documented historically. It has already been shown that the superintendency evolved as a position that functioned at the whims of lay school boards. While the requirements for education and certification narrowed the qualified pool to a select few, the premise under which the superintendency was founded in the first place—to serve as the leader of the local education system at the pleasure of the school board—has not been lost over time.

Laws were developed to direct the process of selecting a superintendent and some consistency was established among many states. As a standard, state regulations stipulated to the local school boards that the selection of the superintendent was the single most important act they would undertake, and that is usually still considered the case (Sharp & Walter, 2004). An important element related to the board's responsibility in selecting a superintendent lies in the fact that the board can, through its selection, have its program or philosophy carried forward. In this regard, it should be noted that the duties of the superintendent are largely determined by the actions of the school board.

The conventional role of the superintendent, as defined by local law in many cases, is to assist the board in formulating and carrying out policy (Carter & Cunningham, 1997). There are, however, some powers conferred upon the superintendent by statute, such as the employment of personnel. And even though school boards are legally prohibited from employing personnel independent of the superintendent's recommendation, they can indeed control the hiring by rejecting the superintendent's recommendations. Therefore, the school board's influence may extend beyond its defined role.

Overall, the job description for a school superintendent tends to be quite broad, including duties that cover almost every aspect of district operations, which isn't surprising considering the chief executive officer is ultimately responsible for all of the district's activities (Kowalski, 1999). While statutes vary from state to state, there are commonalties among the expressed and implied duties of the superintendent, that include:

- Serving as chief executive officer of the school board and thus assuming responsibility for all aspects of the work;
- Providing leadership planning and evaluating all phases of the instructional program;

- Selecting and recommending all personnel to the school board for appointment and guiding the growth of said personnel;
- Preparing the budget for submission to the board and administering it after its adoption;
- Determining building needs and administering building programs, construction, operations, and maintenance; and
- Serving as the leader of the school board, the staff, and the community in improving the education system.

While the general duties of the superintendent are fairly uniform throughout the country, school boards have the option to greatly expand the role and its responsibilities. Also, it is common practice for school boards to have standards or documents defining their own role, thus assisting individual board members in understanding their power and limitations. For example, a standard might point out that an individual board member has no legal powers that are different from any other citizen except when the school board is in session. Further, it is often stated that the school board should see its role as that of a policymaker and the superintendent should administer the school district in accordance with that policy and the legal authority as established by the state. Again, this allows the school board to control the administration of the school district through policies it sets, while giving all legal authority to the superintendent.

Over the decades, the superintendency has long held a reputation for being a difficult profession in which to survive, with a lack of security and many times short tenure. This is the result of numerous factors, including the growing expectations of education by a critical public, the heightened role of employee organizations in administration and policy decisions, and the view that educational leadership is also community leadership. With the increasing awareness of great variations in the presumptions for the superintendency from many different interest groups, the question can be raised about whether the position is not an impossible one. There has been a tendency by many observers, both internally and externally, to regard the superintendent as one who is able to respond to all conflicts, but when conflicts are not resolved to everyone's satisfaction, the superintendent is often soundly condemned.

The school board employs the superintendent to be its chief education officer, and by extension, its advisor, guide, and leader. The teachers, however, often expect the superintendent to support and reflect their points of view in dealing with the board (Hayes, 2001). Citizens who have yet other opinions regarding any number of issues confronting the educational system expect the superintendent to represent their respective views. The bottom line is that each constituent group wants the superintendent to function and make decisions that are in *their* best interest. The superintendent, on the other hand, pledges to make decisions by taking into account the best interests of the students.

The great divide frequently centers on whose definition of "the best interests of the students" is the correct one. It certainly continues to be true that the superintendency is one of the most difficult positions conceivable because so many groups expect so much. Even school board members, some of whom may have been members of the board that first employed the superintendent, often differ in their views regarding the superintendency, and may over time even alter their expectations.

As federal legislation continues to influence the big picture of the future of education in this country, the role of the superintendent becomes more critical and even more tenuous. The superintendent will undoubtedly find himself or herself taking on a different leadership position, not unlike when laws and mandates of the past required courage and unpopular stances to move the agenda forward. When politics would indicate the superintendent needs to seek compromise, he or she is bound by law to implement legislation, even at the risk of being criticized. Usually such requirements place the superintendent at odds with some members of his or her own board, as well as factions of constituent groups.

The school superintendency has evolved into one of the most important positions in our society. Few if any men or women in other professions assume a role that has a greater impact upon the development of individuals and our society. The values held by the superintendent, as well as his or her knowledge, impinge upon many people. It is quite possible that the superintendency has become a position wherein the role is too large, with duties too widespread, for any one person in a school district to handle (Sharp & Walter, 2004).

Generally it is accepted that the superintendent should have broad authority granted by the school board and be held accountable for the effectiveness of the system. When the superintendent does not succeed, in the opinion of the majority of the board, whether or not such is due to circumstances beyond his or her control, the superintendent is often disciplined or dismissed. The risks are high that at some point the superintendent will indeed be held accountable for an issue or action over which he or she has no control. When this occurs, the options are few. The superintendent must always operate from principles of integrity, as anything less would be a violation of the office.

The superintendency today has changed significantly since the formative days of the common school movement. Superintendents are now chief executive officers responsible for multimillion dollar organizations. They are expected to be adept in the political process and in their interactions with state legislative bodies and federal policymakers. As a matter of survival, superintendents must also be expert in the art of internal and external relations as they deal with demanding employees and an increasingly critical public. The days of stoking the furnace and driving the bus have been replaced with the need to be a master in dealing with a school board that often rejects or does not understand its role. As America has progressed from a rural, agrarian environment to urban centers, so has the superintendency. History teaches us that the evolution is ongoing. The definition of the modern superintendency changes as time marches on.

2

Paths to the Superintendency

It is generally assumed that colleges and universities are the institutions that prepare individuals for the superintendency. That view still holds today, with some noted qualifications. Besides formal training, ascension to the superintendency may be influenced by sponsorship, mentorship, and politics.

In the 19th century, when the superintendent was merely an overseer from the ranks of a school committee (Owen & Ovando, 2000), it was mostly personal interest which led an individual to accept the supervisory responsibility. As stated earlier, it was not expected that members of the lay committee had backgrounds as educational experts, let alone were educational leaders. After all, it was the principal in those days who was the actual school administration specialist. The increasing importance of the position of school superintendent ushered in the need for more of an education professional. Again, this first professional was generally a layperson from the committee who had a strong interest in the supervision of schools.

One phenomenon that followed the supervisor of schools era was the accession of the most visible and often the most vocal school figure to leadership positions—the coach. The coaches of major sports teams such as football and basketball, along with band directors, were often seen as good leaders. This was especially true if they were popular with the general population and were winners in their respective fields. It was often taken for granted that leadership transferred from one venue to another. And indeed it was, given the fact that coaches and band directors were found in principalships all across the country in the early 20th century. Formal training at universities that offered courses in educational administration and supervision often followed these favored appointments.

The organizational structures that developed leadership at lower levels in education systems produced administrators who rose through the ranks to become professional superintendents. Patterns of high visibility, coupled with a public image as a winner, seemed to be one way to climb the educational leadership leader, and ultimately reach the superintendency. For the most part, these superintendents were promoted from within the districts, where they served as a principal after first holding a position as a classroom teacher. Occasionally these fortuitous administrators were recruited by other nearby school districts that were aware of their reputations as leaders or winners. The majority of the first superintendents had secondary teaching experience (Glass, 2000b) as opposed to elementary teaching experience. Eventually, the typical route to the superintendency included a stint in the central office after first serving as a building principal and a successful classroom teacher.

Another early path to the superintendency was sponsorship, which is sometimes loosely referred to as the "old boys" network. This sponsorship came in many forms. Some candidates were sponsored by universities and some by professors in educational administration. Others were sponsored by informal networks of leaders in public education who might persuade school district officials that their group held the best superintendent candidates. The old boys network was often difficult to enter, especially for ethnic minorities and women. Occasionally there was word that a woman or two was particularly talented and should be allowed into the club. Once in, the sponsored persons were dutifully shepherded into available positions. Data suggests that men were more likely to be sponsored by universities and state level organizations while most women were sponsored by consultants whom they had come to know based on their high profile and extraordinary work in the field of educational leadership.

Another avenue that has played a crucial part in the careers of school administrators—especially those who ultimately became superintendents—was mentoring. While sponsorship involves being assisted or promoted by others who have influence and power in the area of job placement and has political overtones, mentoring is thought of as more of a professional relationship in which an influential practitioner shares knowledge and guides career advancement (Kowalski, 1999). Mentors for preservice educational administration programs tend to be either practicing or former superintendents (Björk & Keedy, 2001), and mentoring itself can provide an important link between academic training and practical job application (Glass, 1992).

In this situation, the aspiring superintendent would make it known that his or her career goal was to be a superintendent. Concomitant to this clear established direction was the need to be accepted by a mentor from whom the aspirant could learn. This informal, or in some cases formal training, generally happened within the same district where the protégé was employed. It was also helpful if the aspiring superintendent was already in a responsible, high-level position, particularly at the central office. Occasionally mentoring extended below the central office to the principalship, especially in smaller school districts. One danger in this scenario of preordainment is the possibility that it will backfire if the mentoring superintendent experiences trouble. By association, the problem may rub off on the protégé. In such cases the aspirant often has the difficult task of convincing the powers that be that he or she is not like the superintendent or tied to the problem. Regardless of whether the aspirant is successful in ascending to the internal top post, mentoring is still very powerful. The protégé will have learned valuable skills that are transportable to other school districts that may need a talented superintendent.

A more controversial route to the superintendency that has not been well chronicled is political appointment. While the literature is mostly silent on this kind of ascension, it is clear to even the casual observer of educational leadership paths that political maneuvering does occur with some candidates in their quest for the superintendency. An aspirant in such circumstances, whether qualified for the position or not, would bypass conventional methods of demonstrating competence and opt instead to seek favor with the power brokers. The power brokers, for the most part, would be members of the school board who were in the majority. The method often used by the political aspirant was to seek enough votes to attain the superintendency when it became vacant. While the candidate was often successful in this kind of political maneuvering, the danger was that the actions and activities that won the job would be fairly transparent to all who were observing the individual. Ultimately, these political appointees spent a great deal of time counting votes and looking over their shoulders to see who may be working against them. Another risk in this kind of self-aggrandizing behavior is the alienation of colleagues or subordinates who will be reluctant to place their trust and confidence in a new superintendent who attained the position through political appointment. The appointed superintendent is rarely successful in gaining the long-term credibility and respect needed to serve with dignity.

The preparation of today's superintendent could come as a result of any one of the various methods just discussed, or it could be a combination of methods that brings the aspirant to the top post. About half of the superintendents responding to a survey in a 10-year study by the American Association of School Administrators (AASA) say that the old boys network still exists (Glass, et al., 1992), but 78 percent consider themselves to be mentors to others interested in the superintendency as a career, and almost 60 percent said they were assisted by a mentor (Glass, 2000d). Yet the method of preparation that has become the most typical for the superintendency is college and university training programs.

Several colleges and universities in the United States have an educational leadership component within their education graduate programs. These generic, traditional, degree-granting programs purport to prepare administrators for various levels of responsibility, including the superintendency. Obviously, with the range of options available for training administrators, there are different degrees of success. Nevertheless, these traditional training programs continue to be the most direct route to state certification, which is a major ticket to getting the job.

Even as college and university training programs continue to be the main route for ascension, they have frequently been criticized for inadequately preparing individuals to become successful superintendents. Preparation programs for school administrators have been called fragmented, unfocused, and lacking a carefully sequenced curriculum. University-trained administrators support such claims, vocalizing the inadequacy of the preparation through institutions as it relates to the realities of the work of the superintendency, with poor and irrelevant course work (Glass, 1992), too much emphasis on theory, and a faculty out of touch with practice (Kowalski, 1999). In the last three 10-year surveys conducted by the AASA (1982, 1992, and 2000), when superintendents were asked to rank the top three weaknesses of university-based preparation programs, they gave the same answers each time: lack of hands-on application, inadequate access to technology, and failure to link content to practice (Björk 2001).

Interestingly, some researchers have found that superintendents have generally been satisfied with their university-based preparation programs (Björk, 2000b). National 10-year surveys of superintendents conducted by the AASA in 1982 (Cunningham and Hentges), 1992 (Glass), and 2000 (Glass, et al.) have reported that more than 70 percent of superintendents regarded their professional preparation as either good or excellent, and that includes superintendents who received their highest degree within five years of the 2000 survey. Other studies of superintendents and educational administration professors have confirmed those findings. A 1987 study conducted by the National Center for Educational Information found that superintendents were generally pleased with their university-based training (Brunner & Björk, 2001), as did Chapman's (1997) study of beginning superintendents, which also found that more than 86 percent rated their university-based preparation as either good or excellent.

Yet 62 percent of the superintendents who responded to the 2000 AASA survey had completed their degrees and/or licensure programs before the educational reform movement of the 1980s (Björk, 2000b), which may account for their perceptions of the quality of their university-based programs.

The most recent 10-year study of superintendents by the AASA found that a majority of superintendents completed their professional licensure programs more than a decade before being asked to evaluate their experiences, with 40 percent reporting that they received their highest degree more than 15 years prior (Björk, 2001). Of course their views do not relate to the preparation programs needed for future superintendents (Glass, 2000a). And despite their perceptions, studies conducted over the last few decades do show that superintendents are being challenged by different working conditions, and critics report widespread dissatisfaction among those who are completing graduate degree or certification programs in educational administration (Björk, 2000b).

During the 1980s and early 1990s, education administration programs were reviewed by national commissions and task forces (Björk, 2001). The initiatives are supported by numerous reports and position papers. Examples include the reports of the National Commission on Excellence in Educational Administration (1987) and the National Policy Board for Educational Administration (1989). The latter came in the form of a work entitled *Improving the Preparation of School Administrators: An Agenda for Reform*. In summary, the reports highlighted the inadequacies of the ideology and organization of university curricula designed to prepare school system leaders. Many groups detailed the problems and provided suggestions for improvement. Overall, the reports clarified the relationships between effective school reform and administrator preparation, and examined administration licensure programs. In addition, they criticized prevailing practices and issued key recommendations for restructuring professional preparation in the field by strengthening field connections, revising courses, modifying instruction, integrating clinical practice with instruction, and recruiting student cohorts (Björk, 2001). Another important outcome of discussing leadership and superintendent preparation is recognizing the increased political nature of the job and acknowledging the need for superintendents to acquire skills to work more effectively in that context in both schools and communities (Björk, 2000a).

Since the 1980s, a number of major efforts have been made to improve college programs leading to superintendent certification. Although many states are requiring much more preparation for their school administrators, most states and universities only have an extended principal preparation program and none designed specifically for superintendents. However the major national organizations that represent administrators have been working to set up their own superintendency programs (Hayes, 2001). Professional organizations such as the AASA and the National Policy Board for Educational Administration have been ardent critics of upholding the status quo. They have advocated a larger role for practitioners within the profession—to have a stronger voice in defining standards, as well as contributing to the design and implementation of preparation programs that emphasize executive skill development and include all of the scholarly requirements, along with high-quality direct experience.

National standards for the superintendency as a profession were developed by the National Commission on Professional Standards for the Superintendency, a group sponsored by AASA, and published in 1993 (Hoyle, 1993). The standards, which outline professional requirements in eight specific areas, are to be used as guidelines by board members, as well as benchmarks for a superintendent's professional preparation and licensing (Kowalski & Glass, 2002), and ongoing professional development (Carter & Cunningham, 1997). In addition, the AASA, the National Association of Elementary School Principals, and the National Association of Secondary School Principals, along with a coalition of national groups formed the Interstate School Licensure Coalition (ISSLC) to improve programs for school administrators. The ISSLC created a test for evaluating administrative degrees and certifying candidates. Only a few states have adopted the test so far, but others are considering it (Hayes, 2001). While not all states license school superintendents, those that do are moving in the direction of upgrading licensing standards, especially those pertaining to lifelong licenses. The trend is toward requiring all educators, including superintendents, to continue with their professional development (Kowalski, 1999).

Other responses to the need for structural change and the melding of theory and practice have been developed over the years. One is the Cooperative Superintendency Program, located at the University of Texas Department of Educational Administration at Austin. This program was developed as a faculty response to criticism in Texas about weak programs for training school system leaders. The Cooperative Superintendency Program identifies a prospective pool of applicants annually from a national talent search, using scientifically-based, rigorous selection criteria. From selection to graduation, these Superintendent Fellows follow a two-year cycle of instruction. After successfully completing a program of intensive study and research, combined with an internship in a school management position, Superintendent Fellows are granted a doctorate. They then return to the profession of educational leadership with the expectation that they will rapidly rise through the ranks to the top of the field, and the superintendency (Estes, 2002).

Another program is the Urban Superintendents Program at the Harvard Graduate School of Education. The Harvard program offers a doctoral degree designed specifically for those who wish to transform education as superintendents of our nation's urban school systems. The Urban Superintendents Program is a rigorous course of study designed for professionals who have worked innovatively and effectively in metropolitan school districts as teacher-leaders, school principals, or central office administrators. This program clearly is a response to the dearth of high-level training for school leaders in urban centers. The program features course work, an internship, and the research and writing of a dissertation. Individuals who choose the Urban Superintendents Program are basically committed to becoming astute coalition builders, expert managers of human and financial resources, and scholar-practitioners for some of our nation's most challenging school systems (Peterkin, 2002).

Both of these programs represent an approach to filling the need to go beyond the traditional graduate training program for educational administration leadership. They are highly successful and have been around for more than a dozen years. Each year the programs are reviewed for effectiveness, and standards are set to improve the intensity and support consistent with the needs of the marketplace and the students. Programs like the Cooperative Superintendency Program and the Urban Superintendents Program deserve serious consideration for replication by other institutions throughout the country.

Another program, which is newer and found at a smaller university in the Midwest, is the Center for Educational Executives at Aurora University in Aurora, Illinois. The Center, which was developed following discussions with local, state, and national school leaders, is dedicated to enhancing and preparing competent and qualified executive school leaders who are seeking exceptional leadership development experiences. The focus is on providing leadership development experiences that are rich in personal assessment and feedback, and designed to stimulate growth that will assist participants in becoming more successful and productive. The strength of the program is its strong emphasis on practitioner success modeling. Individuals who participate in the various Center activities can evaluate their own leadership styles and receive guidance in developing realistic, practical, and effective plans for personal and professional growth from some of the most successful school executives in the country. Opportunities through the Center—like its predecessor counterparts at the University of Texas and Harvard University—include participating as one of a select group of Superintendent Fellows. These Fellows are chosen for their potential as future school superintendents, and matriculate through the Aurora University College of Education doctoral program. At or near the completion of the program, the Superintendent Fellows are assisted by

Aurora University and its partners in placement as superintendents across the state of Illinois and beyond.

The three programs just described actually intersect two cultures, practice and academia, which are each created with different sets of values. In practice, effective leadership is acknowledged and rewarded accordingly. In the world of academia, recognition is based on achieving excellence in standards of scholarship and research productivity. Are tensions likely to continue between these seemingly incompatible cultures? Research suggests that neither formal knowledge nor concrete experience is enough for optimal learning and transfer. However, the interaction between the two elements provides a powerful vehicle for achieving both. Thus, well-known scholars and practitioners are calling for a blending of theory and practice in university and local school district environments (Björk & Keedy, 2001). The current discussion in the field focuses on integrating knowledge and practice preparation by reconnecting the academic with the practical (Björk, 2001), relying on instructors who have a real sense of what a superintendent's work is all about, as well as a grounding in the academics of school administration (Björk, 2000b).

There is a consensus among superintendents that professional preparation programs must be redesigned to confront the problems that face school administrators (Björk, 2000a). Superintendents do believe that preparation and training programs could be substantially improved. In particular, they could be better coordinated, contain more practical experience, and extend to later professional development (Glass, 1992). While the concerns for the preparation of future school system leaders seem to be common, the reconciliation of the practice-theory dichotomy remains difficult for most institutions of higher learning. To maintain the status quo is unacceptable. But change will require a serious reconceptualization of administrator preparation programs that extends well beyond simply tinkering with graduate administration preparation programs, to accommodate both the existing cultures and structures within our institutions of higher learning and the true reality of the work of a superintendent. For when it comes to nonuniversity based professional preparation and training programs, almost 25 percent of the superintendents surveyed regard course content and the ability of the instructor to relate content to practice as the greatest strengths (Björk, 2000b).

Heightened concern for school reform is adding to the sense of urgency to restructure educational administration and in-service education programs. It is creating the spark for discussions involving a wide range of providers—universities, schools, and professional associations—to form partnerships, collaborations, coalitions, and networks, and to share in the responsibility for professional preparation of school and district administrators. It will also determine how the next generation of superintendents will be recruited, prepared, selected, and provided with in-service education (Björk & Keedy, 2001).

3

Laying the Groundwork for Success

A newspaper in a Wisconsin city in 2002 reported on a superintendent who was calling it quits after 19 years. He was quoted in the story as stating: "I didn't move into the superintendent's position to be involved in politics and labor negotiations, I wanted to be involved in educating kids." This story is not unique, as superintendents across the country are leaving their positions at an alarming rate, through early retirements or a job or career change, just to get out. In one survey of urban superintendents, 98 percent called being a superintendent a "high-stress and high-visibility job." Some cited the essence of the problem as a discrepancy between intentions and resources, or unrealistic expectations of what schools can accomplish (Farkas, et al., 2003). Superintendents must clearly understand their environment, the role they are expected to play, and the types of schools that are necessary today before they can provide the leadership that is needed in the 21st century (Carter & Cunningham, 1997). The expectations and the requirements for the job need to be established so that future superintendents may be successful and this drama is not continually repeated.

As chief executive officers, superintendents occupy key positions in our nation's schools. Many are responsible for huge budgets and large numbers of diverse employees. However unlike CEOs in many private companies, superintendents cannot single-handedly take on new missions and objectives (Kowalski, 1999). And because external forces and authorities influence the administration of a public school system, superintendents often face different and more complicated challenges than do the heads of private organizations (Shibles, et al., 2001). Superintendents must contend with surroundings that contain a blend of state and local authority, political and economic constraints, needs of students and the community, and idealistic notions of professionalism and democracy. Adding to that are issues such as poverty, illegal drugs, and violence, which make a superintendent's job even more demanding (Kowalski, 1999). Not only are superintendents held accountable for decisions and outcomes, they must show results. But the public, as their judge, often does not agree on what those results should be (Shibles, et al., 2001).

Yet superintendents do exert substantial influence on the direction of curriculum and delivery of instruction. A study commissioned by the Wallace Foundation and conducted by the University of Minnesota and the University of Toronto looked at how leadership practices, approaches, and policies impacted student learning (2004). According to their preliminary findings, principals and superintendents have an indirect but powerful influence on student learning. Among school-related factors, only the quality of classroom instruction had a greater effect (Education Commission of the States, 2005). So although they are usually far removed from the classroom, the actions of superintendents can and do affect student performance.

School systems are in need of visionary, creative, and passionate leaders. They need superintendents who have a clear understanding of their organization's purpose, and a realistic comprehension of their organization's capacity to achieve its purpose. Moreover, school systems need superintendents who can lead schools to be effective even when human and financial resources are in short supply.

Believing that the superintendency today is structured for the purpose of being directly involved with the education of students falls far short of reality. Most superintendents come from the teaching ranks and usually move through preparatory chairs before ascending to the superintendency.

For this reason alone, it is not unusual to find that superintendents work hard to positively affect the education of students. This is a lofty outlook, if it can be achieved. However in today's environment in most school systems, success as a superintendent requires many other types of skills. Legislative and judicial acts, and a growing demand for constituents to determine how a school district is run, have created almost impossible demands on the superintendent. This individual must juggle the roles of politician, educator, and manager so that the community is satisfied, students get educated, employees are happy, and the district continues to be financially stable (Owen & Ovando, 2000).

A key to success as a superintendent, whether he or she is new to the profession or the position, is to work with constituents to identify the education vision for the school system. *Vision* can be defined as the mental image of an organization's past and it's ideal future (Kowalski, 1999). Vision sets the direction and helps maintain focus, especially in school districts where there is a continual push to add more to the list. *Mission*, on the other hand, is more specific; it describes the work that needs to be done by the organization to make the vision happen (Townsend, et al., 2005). The education vision includes the district's beliefs about students, learning, teaching, employee and community organizations, governance, management, parents, and other internal and external relationships. In the best-case scenario, this is already well established, and all that the new superintendent has to do is study the existing structure and stay the course. But even in the best case, where the incumbent is revered and admired, it is advisable for a new leader to undertake certain important steps.

It is a good idea for a superintendent to learn about the community and the organization before recommending an appropriate course of action (Owen & Ovando, 2000). New superintendents spend much of their initial time gathering information through a structured process (Chapman, 1997). The first step for a new superintendent is to meet with groups of people—such as staff members, business and civic leaders, community members at large, and parents—and really listen to how they express their core beliefs about various aspects of education. These groups will generally have different ideas about the many facets of the school system. As basic as it sounds, listening is the primary skill the superintendent needs in these multiple meetings (Hayes, 2001). Displaying an open mind and listening, rather than steering the conversation, or being tempted to evoke personal beliefs, will usually produce patterns with common threads that run through the groups. Being attentive and taking copious notes will win points for the new superintendent as well. By the time this phase is completed, the superintendent will have met with hundreds of people. All of these meetings and discussions should help a new administrator draw up a plan for improving the district (Hayes, 2001).

The community's own vision for the district may not agree with that of the superintendent's. And while visionary superintendents intend to educate the community and propel the district forward, a vision that appears to ignore the community's culture and desires may not be feasible. Without including the perspectives of different constituents, there is a risk of presenting a vision that does not reflect what the community wants (Johnson, 1996). It is the superintendent's responsibility to ensure that whatever actions are taken are in alignment with the core values of the schools (Carter & Cunningham, 1997); community values must be respected in setting the direction for the district because the schools belong to the community (Owen & Ovando, 2000).

The next phase is to schedule a retreat with all members of the school board, which is the most effective way to get board members thinking about their governing structure (Houston & Eadie, 2002). The first order of business is for the superintendent to share with them what he or she has learned from the district's constituents. This presentation should occur in a relaxed setting, but with a structured format. A good approach would be to obtain permission from the board to lead the entire first part of the retreat. In this first session, the superintendent needs to structure the presentation so that the categories of core beliefs are clearly understood by board members. The presentation should proceed with the superintendent walking the board through the meetings that were held with the various constituent bodies. An outline of patterns that were found when interacting with the groups should be well organized and clearly stated. Handled correctly, this exercise with the board may take several hours, as the superintendent reveals the findings and other details that led to the conclusions being made.

In the second half of the meeting, the superintendent should work with the board to develop a common vision for the district utilizing information from the first presentation. Working as a team, the superintendent should encourage board members to surface their beliefs, assumptions, and values about education before discussing and agreeing on common purposes for the schools in their district (Shibles, et al., 2001). A good approach would be to ask each board member to privately write a specified number of belief statements about the core areas on a blank sheet of paper without discussing it with the other members. The next task is to have board members openly share their written belief statements with their colleagues. This process needs to be structured so that each board member shares information while the others listen. The various statements can be posted around the room as the board members reveal them to the group. Ultimately, through discussion, some statements will merge with others while some will be eliminated. This entire exercise should be conducted in an atmosphere of mutual respect and trust.

One method that could then be employed is to have the board decide up front how many belief statements should be targeted. By the end of the one-or two-day retreat, the board will have agreed on a vision and set of core beliefs for the school system. The beauty of this method is that clear input from the constituent groups obviously will have influenced the board in its deliberations. By following this exercise, the board and superintendent can agree on realistic goals and steps for achieving the expectations for the district. Information gained from this process can further be used to form board policies and actions.

Helping the board to identify and articulate criteria on which they will base future judgments is a critical task for the superintendent. This essential step establishes a foundation for all future decisions. Without a guiding purpose or a vision, boards tend not to set a policy agenda and instead consider issues on an ad hoc basis. Superintendent-board partnerships that have criteria distinctly spelled out to guide their decision making are able to communicate and implement their policies more effectively (Shibles, et al., 2001). The final outcome of the process can be communicated in a document that includes measurable objectives that will serve as a tool for evaluating the performance of the superintendent. The result is that the superintendent will have established himself or herself as a listener, and set the stage for success as the leader of the school district.

Another purpose of the retreat, and possibly as important to the superintendent personally as any other planning which has occurred up to this point, is establishing a common understanding of the relationship between the school board and the superintendent (Houston & Eadie, 2002). One of the standards developed by the American Association of School Administrators (AASA) for superintendents relates to roles and relationships. It states that "superintendents should develop procedures for working with the board that specify mutual expectations, working relationships, and strategies for formulating district policy for external and internal programs" (AASA, 1994).

The extent to which the superintendent and school board work together has tremendous impact on anything else that takes place in the school system. And certainly a good relationship between them should not be assumed or taken for granted. On the contrary, of all the issues that can lead to problems in a district, the roles of the board and the superintendent may be the most heated (Hayes, 2001). Often an antagonistic relationship with the board—whether because of role conflict (Glass, 2000d) or lack of support (Carter & Cunningham, 1997)—is the primary reason that leads to superintendents leaving the district for another position.

The future relationship between the superintendent and the school board should also be purposely planned. The best way to begin the discussion about superintendent and school board relations is to make sure that all board members express their opinions about this issue verbally. This is important because it is possible that some board members may not know where their colleagues stand on this topic. In an earlier discussion leading up to the retreat, the superintendent and the school board president should plan the structure for this particular exercise that gives board members an opportunity to express their opinions. Depending on the situation and the comfort level of the board president, the exercise should be led by the school board. The superintendent should contribute to the discussion only when the board feels the need for the superintendent to be involved. In other cases the process may be more effective if the board president and the superintendent facilitate the discussion as a team.

However it is structured, each board member should be asked to define a good superintendent-school board relationship. Throughout their deliberation, issues related to the roles of the school board and the superintendent should surface. Unless the school board is completely dysfunctional, the results will yield a mutual understanding of the appropriate roles for the superintendent and the school board, and their ideal relationship. With proper and skilled processing of this issue by the board president and/or the superintendent, the agreement on the relationship between the school board and the superintendent should be similar to what the state and national school board associations espouse. The National School Boards Association and other state associations have formed guidelines for board members (Sharp & Walter, 2004) to reduce role conflict and confusion (Kowalski, 2001). The wise superintendent will read and become familiar with these documents and share the same with school board members well in advance of the retreat.

Aside from participating in shaping the agreement, the superintendent should take the opportunity to tell school board members what they can expect from him or her. The atmosphere created by the previous discussions will allow for frankness on the part of the superintendent that might not be tolerated at another time or in a different setting. The superintendent should pledge to board members that they can expect and rely on "no surprises" when it comes to communicating information (Houston & Eadie, 2002; Hoyle, et al., 2005), meaning the school board will hear important news directly from the superintendent. This pledge should be backed up with a plan for how it will be accomplished.

Regardless of the size of a district, there are ways for the superintendent to conduct his or her business so that the school board is always kept informed on matters relating to the school district. As a matter of good communication, the school board should never learn about important or critical school district issues via "the grapevine" or the news media; the superintendent should convey such information to school board members personally. Examples can be as simple as a bus fender bender with no injuries, a bomb scare at one of the schools, or a weapon confiscated from a student. More traumatic issues might be a bus incident where students were taken to hospitals, or a shooting at a school. Whatever the issue, the superintendent should have a procedure in place for notifying individual school board members immediately, before it becomes public knowledge (Hayes, 2001). This can be accomplished through telephone calls or a voice mail system set up by the school district specifically for board members to access on a daily basis.

The discussion of no surprises can also extend to include school board members and their responsibility to promptly notify the superintendent about crises or even rumors which may come to their attention, or it may be brought up at an earlier point.

In addition to the superintendent pledging to inform board members promptly about anything school district related, he or she should promise to provide board members with a weekly written report on the status of the school district. If the school board meets formally once per month, then one of the weekly reports can be included with the meeting agenda and background material mailed to board members. Should the school board meet more often, communications can be consolidated with the regular agendas and background materials for the meetings. Whatever the case, the weekly report is a good tool for ongoing communication with the school board.

Another important understanding should focus on how the superintendent will communicate with individual board members who might telephone the superintendent directly with a question. It should be established that such questions will be answered to the best of the superintendent's knowledge. If the superintendent does not have an immediate answer but can obtain a response without time consuming research, he or she should call the school board member back with the information. However, should the question require in-depth research, which ultimately takes the form of creating a written document, or requires complex retrieval of documents that are ordinarily not available, then all school board members should receive a copy, along with the question that resulted in creating a written response. This procedure will serve to prevent individual school board members from revealing at a public meeting internal documents received from the superintendent that other school board members do not have. It will also keep school board members from playing the game of one-upmanship with their fellow board members. While this type of discussion may be delicate for the superintendent, it is important to be held early in the superintendent's employment, and in a safe environment such as a retreat. The last thing a superintendent needs is to confront any of these issues during a time of crisis and have to create rules for handling them after the fact.

As vital as it is to have good communications with the school board, the successful superintendent will have a plan for good internal communication with staff and other school district employees. While good external communications are extremely important, and ultimately may define the superintendent as a leader, employees should not have to rely on public media or other external sources for information about the district. Therefore, it is absolutely essential that the superintendent establish a good internal communications strategy. Again, the size of the school district will dictate the kinds of communication strategies that are needed. In small districts, there should be regular meetings between the superintendent and the administrative leaders. And if the total employee force is fewer than one hundred, the superintendent may want to hold several meetings throughout the year with all of the employees present to update them on the state of the district.

In a larger district, it may be impractical to meet with all of the district's employees or faculty members at one time, and the superintendent may have to divide the employees and/or faculty into smaller groups for the desired face-to-face communication. Either way, the facts remain the same: It is important to have direct communication between the superintendent and individuals who are employed by the school system. In larger districts, various strategies can be employed with the administrative leadership to foster good communication. Principals and central office administrators can meet with the superintendent as a group two or three times per year, while a smaller representative body meets with the superintendent on a weekly or monthly basis to keep the lines of communication open between the superintendent and the rest of the administrative staff. Whichever method is used, the internal administrative staff should feel valued by the superintendent's actions to meet with them on some consistent basis and to keep them informed about school system issues.

External relations by the superintendent, on the other hand, require skillful and regular engagement with the public. If the public was only involved in the initial portion of the visioning process, the superintendent will have failed. To abandon the public after using them for a specific purpose is tantamount to giving them false hope and promise for the future. Following discussions with the school board and internal leaders on the staff, plans should be developed to create ongoing, sustaining relationships with the public in an attempt to include the input of everyone in the district's external audience. Engaging the public should be considered an investment in the district and the community (Cambron-McCabe, et al., 2005). The main idea behind engaging the public is to inspire the public to "own" its schools. If that sense of ownership is not instilled, the public's support may not be forthcoming when it is needed (Pendleton & Benjamin 2005).

Again, the superintendent must be cognizant of the district's community and its sub-communities. While it may be difficult to contemplate segmenting the community into groups of similar interests, it could pay big dividends. Advisory groups, made up of very specific segments of the community, can be a valuable way to collect district information (Hoyle, et al., 2005). The superintendent, for example, could purposely develop an advisory group made up of local clergy. Thus, there would be no need to scramble to seek advice that only the clergy could give in a time of crisis because the system for communication with the right group would already be in place.

The same structure can be repeated for groups such as senior citizens, realtors, business leaders, and students. If there are defined ethnic or racial groups in the district, it is a very positive move to develop advisory groups wherein they can meet and discuss issues with the superintendent that are unique to their interests. Ultimately, the discussion will go beyond just the issues that are common to their group and include broader discussions, which are important to the school district as a whole.

The same opportunity for interaction and reflection should be accorded to groups such as unions and employee associations. Although these groups are often viewed as part of the internal structure, the nature of their work would require that they be given the same treatment and respect as other significant and important members of the public. While these special interest groups are excellent tools for keeping the public informed about the school system on a regular basis, they allow the superintendent to stay tuned in to the real issues in the district. And as a bonus, the superintendent builds a tremendous support base by nurturing meaningful engagement with the public.

After the vision and mission for the district are established, it is time to go to work and align school system operations with the direction set by the school board based on the input of the various publics. This stage of development is best handled by working with specific leaders on the administrative staff. Regardless of the size of the district, a body of advisors from the ranks of the administrative staff can be helpful in recommending the framework for implementation. In larger districts, the appropriate staff advisors would be the body that is often referred to as the superintendent's cabinet, the superintendent's staff, the executive staff, the executive team, or often the senior staff. These are the people who meet regularly with the superintendent and work as a team in advising the superintendent on any number of issues. A small district may want to tap a select group of leaders to create a leadership team that will process the vision and mission information and advise the superintendent on steps for implementation. In either case, work sessions should be scheduled to develop the implementation plan.

The resulting document for implementation is sometimes referred to as the *program of work*. The program of work essentially looks at the big picture, as expressed by the vision and mission, and divides it into workable parts with detailed implementation steps. Those steps can lead to initiatives such as reorganizing the central administrative staff, restructuring grade level configurations, redefining the school day, or any number of new directions which are supported by the system's new vision and mission. It is important to stress throughout this examination process that the district's action must be consistent with its philosophy as expressed through its vision and mission statements.

The bottom line is to align the organization to support what the school district's constituents believe is important. Ultimately, the program of

work will outline very clearly the direction of the district and the method needed to achieve the desired results.
School systems that are led by superintendents with vision are the systems that will do well on most fronts.

An unambiguous and suitable vision, along with an understandable plan for change, can concentrate the efforts of teachers, administrators, and community members as they move forward to improve their schools. Inviting others to envision change as well, demonstrates to the district and the community that the superintendent realizes the community's stake in its education system, and the role that is appropriate for the superintendent as its leader. By involving a broad range of interests in developing a vision, the superintendent ensures that those same people will be committed to seeing the vision through (Johnson, 1996).

If improving student achievement is the issue, as it is in so many districts across the country, then improvement plans can be developed and measured against the district vision and mission, and steps can be defined in the program of work to achieve the goal. Superintendents who are organized in this manner can also use the visioning process to guide any number of day-to-day or long-term decisions. In the end, it is the job of the superintendent to find as many ways as possible to instill staff, parent, community, and even student commitment to the system's vision and core beliefs. To accomplish this, people at all levels of the organization need to be inspired.

The superintendent's vision in and of itself will have a minimal effect in promoting improvement in education unless everyone in the district understands it, believes it has meaning, and realizes what it holds in store for them (Johnson, 1996). The impetus for change, along with the security of the superintendent's position, is broadened as more interest groups take on roles in the education process. Although the superintendent has the authority to institute change, the real power comes from the support of the district's stakeholders (Carter & Cunningham, 1997).

Superintendents who succeed in building and maintaining their district through this kind of systematic leadership will, by and large, stay the course and not be swayed by every fad that comes along as the flavor of the day for effective leadership. Involving others in meaningful ways, and following through, is not magic. One simply has to recognize that visionary leadership for restructuring and improving school systems is possible for the serious superintendent. The call is for district leaders to connect the community around a common vision for the schools and structure their leadership and the system around that vision (Institute for Educational Leadership, 2001). The superintendency may be a demanding position, but by following proper procedures and being sensitive to community sentiment and values, the chances of success are dramatically improved (Owen & Ovando, 2000).

PART II
Mastery of the Profession

4

Superintendent-School Board Relations

Most superintendents understand that their relationship with the school board is a major key to their survival, as well as their ability to provide effective leadership. Ninety-six percent of the superintendents polled in one survey agreed that their relationship with the board is crucial in making important educational decisions (Cooper, et al., 2000). Leading and governing a school district requires that a school board and superintendent form and maintain a productive partnership. While the board and the superintendent have separate roles and functions, each depends upon the other to be successful (Danzberger, 1998). Without a solid partnership with the board, a superintendent's authority will be undermined as the board second-guesses decisions, and may very well lead to the superintendent's dismissal (Eadie, 2003).

Many superintendents have experienced how impossible the job becomes when board relations begin to deteriorate. Among the reasons why superintendents lose their jobs, relationships seem to surface as the major factor (Carter & Cunningham, 1997). There are no pat answers in ensuring good relationships, or turning them around once they have soured. However, it is prudent for a superintendent to acknowledge at the very beginning of his or her employment that relationships could become a problem at any time and to make known the desire to discuss that potential early on. The best approach is to prepare a discussion with the school board to identify processes that are already established or propose developing a strategy to deal with the situation before it happens (Danzberger, 1998).

It would be instructive to comment on the common legal responsibility of school boards across the United States. To have a clear picture of why school boards exist, and to understand what is expected of them with regard to their relationships with superintendents, we need to know what is legally required of both the school board and the superintendent. Legally, school boards are corporate bodies, defined as municipal corporations but more often quasi-corporations (Kowalski, 1999). They receive their authority from the state to oversee school districts (Hoyle, 2005).

Basically, the school board is made up of elected individuals who serve the general voting population within defined school district boundaries. While the number of board members may vary across the country, it is most common that school boards have seven members. Usually the school board is made up of an odd number of members—five, seven, or nine—so that the likelihood of a deadlock is minimized, assuming that all members are present for voting. In many ways, the school board functions like the board of directors of a corporation (Sharp & Walter, 2004). Like a corporate board, individual board members do not have the power to make decisions (Kowalski, 2001). The board must take action as a committee, and the majority rules. The superintendent cannot veto the board's decisions. If there are issues on which the board and the superintendent cannot reach a compromise, unless it is something illegal, the board always wins (Sharp & Walter, 2004).

Legislation in most states would indicate that the superintendent of schools is the only direct employee of the school board. All other employees of the school district actually report through the system to the superintendent rather than the school board. Many in the rank and file who sometimes loosely assume that they work for the school board often misunderstand the *single employee of the school board* concept. Another misconception is that certain individuals, such as the auditor, school attorney or architect are direct employees of the school board. While they do work directly for the school board, the actual relationship between the board and these individuals is as service providers rather than employees. Securing and releasing service providers does not involve the due process that is required when employing or dismissing a superintendent. Thus, the superintendent of schools is usually the only direct employee of the school board, and the only person who is legally subject to the employer-employee relationship with the corporate body.

Conventional wisdom would indicate that communication, trust, and understanding role differences are the major factors influencing the effectiveness of a working relationship between the superintendent and the board (Sharp & Walter, 2004). But there is also a legal structure for the school board and for the superintendent's position. In general, school boards have three main duties: 1.) ensure state laws, rules, and regulations regarding education are followed; 2.) set policy in areas that state laws, rules, and regulations do not cover; and 3.) hire a superintendent to act as chief executive officer of the district (Kowalski, 1999). Although laws limit the power of boards to make decisions, boards are allowed to make educational decisions about property taxes for school revenue, school property, employing professional and support staff, and instruction (Hoyle, et al., 2005).

Under the guidance of state law, local boards establish district policy and supervise its implementation by district administrators. The superintendent is typically the school board's chief executive officer (Sharp & Walter, 2004) and is responsible for implementing that policy and overseeing daily district operations. While policy implementation is delegated to local superintendents, the superintendents are expected to make certain that the board and the schools comply with federal and state laws, as well as district policies (Hoyle, et al., 2005). Yet legally and politically, state governments that are responsible for making sure that local school administrators comply with requirements (Kowalski, 2001).

The school board establishes policy and the superintendent carries it out. On its face, that might appear quite simple. Generally it is not that simple or unidirectional (Johnson, 1996), for a variety of reasons. Unlike other district employees, the superintendent must develop and maintain acceptable relations between himself or herself and the school board to be successful. One reason that tends to surface as the main deterrent to good relations is the makeup of the board, and who the board members are as individuals—their background, their level of education, their personality, etc. School boards are now more representative of the community (Glass, 1992); members are essentially lay people who come to the job with no required credentials or formal training (Kowalski, 1999). Their fellow citizens, who in most cases elected them to represent their interests, place them in this position of trust. Thus, board members serve as a link between the community and educators (Sharp & Walter, 2004).

For the most part, board members are required to be of voting age, registered voters, and living within the defined school district boundaries. Once elected, they are entrusted with the responsibility of exercising policymaking power over an institution that is extremely complex. At best, training is available through most state school boards associations (Hayes, 2001). Veteran school board members may also become mentors, providing such veterans understand the true responsibility and functions of a "good" school board member.

The superintendent on the other hand, is a bonafide, credentialed chief executive, who by training and/or experience brings expertise to the office. As a rule, the superintendent is selected for his or her ability, and is not subject to the traditional popularity contests that candidates would endure for an elected office. Yet even with the expertise required to obtain the position and the skills needed to be effective, if school board members do not perceive the superintendent as effective, then he or she is not. In this context, perception is the only reality (Carter & Cunningham, 1997). Therefore, for the superintendent to be successful, he or she must be viewed by the school board in a positive light. Surely a superintendent cannot maintain school board support if members of the board turn against him or her. Because superintendents do not have the protection of tenure, any disagreement that turns a majority of the board against them can lead to their dismissal from the district (Hayes, 2001).

Research and literature are mixed on how well superintendents and school boards really get along. Some sources suggest that "the superintendent and board often work very well together, agreeing most of the time on policy rather than opposing each other" (Sharp & Walter, 2004), while others state that "such relationships are said to be more the exception than the rule" (Shibles, et al., 2001). Strong superintendent-school board relationships based on clear understandings of roles and mutual purpose are the foundation for effective school district governance (Brunner & Björk, 2001). Research on the actions of effective superintendents stresses the value of communication (Glass, 2000a) and good board relationships (Hoyle, et al., 2005). Major factors that stand in the way of productive relationships are role confusion, communication problems, and personal agendas (Carter & Cunningham, 1997). Problems develop when boards and superintendents do not have a thorough understanding of the responsibilities of each side (Sharp & Walter, 2004). Role confusion regarding the board's policymaking duties and the superintendent's administrative function is seen as a prime source of conflict (Owen & Ovando, 2000). Indeed, many authors claim that differing job expectations of boards and superintendents are actually the root cause of the most conflicts (Glass, 2000d).

Members of the same school board may even have different expectations for a superintendent's performance (Kowalski, 1999). Even though states delegate authority to school boards and mandate that they enforce specific laws, at times the boards also may interpret their authority differently, which affects district administration (Sharp & Walter, 2004). While several studies have found that school board members believe communication problems are the biggest reason for conflict between them and the superintendent, in the perception of superintendents it is the attempt of school boards to micromanage school district operations (Norton, et al., 1996). Boards may be charged with the duty of setting policy, but board members don't always agree on how, or even on what policy is, which often moves them toward micromanagement (Shibles, et al., 2001).

It also poses a problem when different groups perceive the superintendent from their points of view. Often, these factions within the school system or community can influence and pressure board members (Sharp & Walter, 2004). In a 10-year survey by the American Association of School Administrators (AASA) in 2000 (Glass, 2000a), over half of the superintendents said community pressure groups try to influence district policy and operations. And of those superintendents in large districts (25,000 plus students) 90 percent report the existence of such pressure groups. Many pressure groups commonly direct their efforts toward both the superintendent and individual board members, which can result in splitting the board (Glass, 1992).

Not only do pressure groups influence board members, but board members themselves may belong to political factions or may be aligned with special interest groups (Institute for Educational Leadership, 2001), which makes the work of the superintendent more difficult (Kowalski, 1999). When board members are elected on special interest platforms, they often tend to promote those interests instead of representing community interests, which creates a fragmented board (Shibles, et al., 2001). According to the 10-year study in 2000 by the AASA, 66 percent of the superintendents surveyed characterized their boards as being actively aligned with community interests, while 19 percent claimed board members represented distinct factions (Björk, 2000a).

The potential for distorted perceptions makes it important for the superintendent to maintain good internal and external communication and gauge the attitude of the public on a regular basis. That includes maintaining relationships with the media, which are also crucial and can be lethal if mishandled. Like most citizens, school board members can be affected by news accounts. We all know that controversy sells, while good news does not usually make the front page. It seems that reporters are also rewarded for covering, or rather uncovering, controversy.

What we have done is set the stage for defining how to establish and maintain good superintendent-school board relations. However, there are a number of further recommendations that can apply, and can increase a superintendent's chances of success in relating to the school board. Although its importance was already mentioned, probably the most valuable suggestion is to communicate with the board on a regular and consistent basis, which is essential for developing and maintaining a successful board relationship (AASA, 1994). Efficient, timely, accurate, and positive communication is not only indispensable to building a trusting relationship with the board, but a superintendent's very survival often depends on it (Kowalski, 2001).

Keeping board members informed about all issues that affect the district—regarding policy development, policy implementation, and community relations—is a primary responsibility of a superintendent (Kowalski, 1999). Board members should never be surprised by hearing about school district business from a source other than the superintendent. It is a great embarrassment for a school board member to hear about an issue in the school district from a citizen who seems to know more than the school board member does. With today's technology, there is no reason not to communicate via voice-mail, e-mail, or fax to get critical information to board members almost instantly. There might even be an occasion when personal and individual telephone calls may be necessary to insure that a message has been delivered. Aside from the immediate notice required to report a crisis, a superintendent should normally communicate in writing with board members at least once per week, detailing issues and events that have been occurring in the school district. To be the most effective, the weekly memorandum should come directly from the superintendent and not a third party. School board members appreciate the superintendent taking the time to personally communicate with them. Remember that the superintendent is the school board's only employee, and board members often thrive on the attention they get from the superintendent.

A second recommendation is for the superintendent to never divide the school board in any way, shape, or form. School boards are seldom united groups anyway, and the superintendent should avoid taking sides (Johnson, 1996). In early discussions with the board about building relationships, it should be understood that the superintendent will treat all school board members equally. The superintendent cannot openly show favoritism to any members of the board (Hayes, 2001). Information that is important to one board member is important to all board members. For example, if one school board member should request that a document be prepared by the superintendent or school staff to assist him or her in understanding the school district or some future action to be taken, the document should be sent to all board members (Sharp & Walter, 2004). The last thing a superintendent needs is for a board member to apply one-upmanship with fellow board members because he or she has information that the others do not, especially if that information was obtained from the superintendent. The superintendent also should not fall into the trap of socializing with some school board members and not others. A better position would be for the superintendent not to be involved in any social situation involving the school board unless it is clearly school district related and all school board members are included. Even though a naive school board member may set up a social situation for select board members, it is the superintendent who will pay the price for participating in the exclusion of the other members.

It goes without saying that a superintendent should always be honest, and not become a pawn of the school board when it comes to espousing professional and personal opinions that would otherwise compromise integrity. School boards tend to respect honesty, forthrightness, and virtue. Consistent behavior along the lines of standing up for principles tends to inspire trust in a superintendent and builds credibility. Likewise, a superintendent needs to be keenly aware of the politics involved in various situations that affect the school board, but avoid becoming a political player. Therefore, care should be taken so as not to be pulled into squabbles that are clearly school board politics because it is too easy for issues to shift from the school board to the superintendent, which could leave the superintendent as the scapegoat or lighting rod.

The superintendent should never withhold information from the board that they have a right to know, and any information should be conveyed in a timely fashion. For example, if the superintendent and board had planned a weekend retreat and the superintendent was made aware of the district losing a substantial amount of money, the superintendent should not wait until after the retreat to avoid having the bad news affect the attitude of the school board members at the retreat. Such logic is flawed, and is a serious mistake on the part of a superintendent who may be attempting to control the atmosphere. The superintendent's credibility in the eyes of the board, and the trust required in that relationship, depends more than anything else on always telling them the full truth—bad news as well as good (Houston & Eadie, 2002).

While the purpose of withholding information in this example was to not allow bad news to influence the tenor of the meeting, it is far better for the superintendent to share the information that the school board had a right to know. As a matter of fact, such missteps would be the kind of ammunition that could be used against a superintendent in the event that the board moves for dismissal. In addition, the superintendent needs to tell the staff that he or she has an obligation to communicate with the school board on all matters that affect the district, and that the board has a right to know about. The staff should likewise cooperate by passing along information to the superintendent of which he or she may not be aware. Then it's up to the superintendent to judge whether or not the information is worth forwarding to the school board. A good rule for the superintendent to follow in such matters is to always pass information on to the board if there is ever a question of its relevance.

Occasionally the information that staff members share with the superintendent will be of a personal nature. When that happens, staff members need to be told by the superintendent that information of a personal nature that may have some bearing on the school system needs to be shared with the school board. Again, the rule is that school board members should never be surprised by feedback they receive from the public about school district issues. And those embarrassing surprises could come in the form of gossip about staff members. While the superintendent should never participate in gossip, he or she has an obligation to pass any factual information on to the school board when it involves staff members.

One example of a personal situation would be if a high-level staff member was arrested on the weekend for driving under the influence of alcohol, and shared the incident with the superintendent the following Monday. The staff member might have spoken with the superintendent under the guise of telling a friend about a personal matter. However, the superintendent should never fall into the trap of allowing staff members to discuss sensitive personal information in that way. While the superintendent is expected to maintain positive relationships with staff members since they are necessary for the success of the superintendency and the school district, the superintendent should be extremely cautious in establishing friendships with staff members that might compromise his or her responsibility to the board. In the case of the DUI confession, the superintendent must carefully explain to the staff member that it is a serious matter, and therefore would be a violation of superintendent-school board relations to conceal such information from the board.

Staff members need to realize that confiding in a friend is quite different from revealing the same information to the superintendent. Staff members should be made aware that the superintendent can never step out of his or her role. Unfortunately, the staff member who received the DUI citation will have to face the consequences of their arrest within the standards established by the school system for handling such matters. A superintendent who would withhold that information from the school board could also face dismissal.

Other issues that come between superintendents and school boards are related to power and control, and are typically manifested in school board members attempting to operate outside of their legal role. For example, board members commonly assume that they are allowed to sponsor individuals for jobs within the school district. This is often played out by school board members overtly or covertly attempting to pressure the superintendent to employ certain applicants that they would like to see hired. Again, the superintendent and school board should discuss such possibilities before they become live examples. The superintendent should make it clear that there is an official process for hiring employees, and the process should not be compromised or influenced by school board members. Yet even in the best discussions and early understanding between the school board and the superintendent, well meaning school board members may hint at whom they think would be a good employee. In those situations, the superintendent should refer the school board member to the established procedure and remain consistent in applying the rules.

Closed meetings of the school board, sometimes referred to as executive sessions, can be another problem area for the superintendent if school board members have a tendency to stray into areas of discussion that are prohibited by law. Most states impose fines and imprisonment if school board members are convicted of violating the open meetings law. The penalties are usually for elected officials and rarely include the superintendent or employees. Notices regarding closed meetings, by law, must be posted in advance, stating the time, place, and purpose. The purpose of the meeting must always be specific and centered on a topic that is allowed by law. Allowable topics generally include: specific personnel matters, such as employee discipline; specific legal matters, for example, pending or imminent litigation; collective bargaining issues with employee groups; discussions of acquisition or disposal of property; and student discipline matters, such as suspension or expulsion. Although the board may discuss such topics in a closed meeting, any decisions must be made during public board meetings (Sharp & Walter, 2004).

The superintendent has a unique responsibility with regard to closed sessions that is different from other employees. As the employee who works directly with the school board, according to the law, the superintendent is expected to be present during all closed sessions. The exception is whenever the school board is scheduled to discuss the employment conditions of the superintendent—including evaluation, compensation, or discipline—or they are meeting to consider dismissal. This requirement, and the possibility of observing board members displaying inappropriate behavior in a closed meeting, places the superintendent in a somewhat awkward position.

It is expected that school board members will obey the law regarding limits on discussion within a closed meeting and not allow any member to violate the rules on what can or cannot be discussed. However, the ethics and/or conduct of school board members are not always aligned from member to member. As a result, the way in which individuals interpret their own actions or responsibility will vary. Yet as a matter of practicality, meeting decorum and the control of discussions falls on the board president. When observed, the president should immediately stop any violations. In a perfect world, a board member may inadvertently stray to a prohibited topic, the president calls attention to the potential violation, and the matter is ended. However, it does not always work that simply. Occasionally a weak board president will allow discussions to wander into prohibited areas. That type of inattention could be attributed to inadequate knowledge or a lack of courage. Either way, school boards often find themselves violating the law by discussing prohibited matters in closed session meetings. Unlike the board president, the superintendent by training has full knowledge of the laws relating to school board meetings. While most laws are silent regarding penalties and fines against the superintendent, there is a clear expectation that the superintendent will not participate in or tolerate violations of the closed meeting laws.

If a superintendent observes violations, he or she must immediately acknowledge them, and through the board president request that the violation cease. This approach will be only as successful as the board president's conviction in dealing with board members who violate the law. Occasions could also arise when the offending board member is the president. In those cases, the superintendent has the same responsibility to acknowledge the violation and request that the discussion cease. Obviously such sensitive observations may strain relationships between the superintendent and the offending board members, but when it comes to upholding the law, the superintendent has no choice.

As difficult as it is for the superintendent to admonish school board members, it may at times be necessary. The degree to which the superintendent will succeed in doing so depends upon the relationship that he or she has established with the board. Having a discussion in advance of any incident is a good way to make sure that the superintendent's position is clear. The best time to talk about the superintendent's role in closed sessions, and how observed violations will be handled, is at a retreat with the board in the beginning of the superintendent's employment. If the superintendent chooses to "look the other way" during a meeting violation, the superintendent's integrity will be on the line. The superintendent can never compromise on professional or personal standards and must establish that fact early on with the board through his or her behavior. In doing so, the superintendent will gain the board's respect for following the law and performing his or her duties with the highest regard for the office.

The superintendent should understand his or her role when it comes to public interaction with the school board as a body or as individuals. Public school board meetings, for example, are forums for school board members, not the superintendent. The chairperson of the meeting is always the school board president and the meetings should be conducted according to Roberts Rules of Order, or a similar procedural process. The superintendent serves as the school board's staff at its public meetings and should never appear to be competing for attention with the board president or any other board member. The superintendent should never make public statements that would embarrass any member of the school board either, as such a mistake is unlikely to be forgiven. Should the superintendent find it necessary to advise a school board member on public errors, it is far better to speak to the school board member in private and very delicately explain the situation. Also, when school board members and the superintendent make community appearances together, it is always wise for the superintendent to defer to board members who seek public recognition.

It is highly unlikely that any superintendent will find him or herself in a position that is completely void of conflict or tension. Unfortunately, there are no really pat answers for handling those situations since they all seem to have a unique twist. It's been said that the best defense is a good offense. Know up front that conflict may occur and be prepared for it. Openly giving examples of situations that could occur to school board members in initial meetings can increase their awareness of the likelihood for conflict. Then when those situations do take place, it is best to proceed with caution and the understanding that school board members are to be treated with care, while at the same time maintaining the integrity of the superintendency. The system will be well served by a superintendent who understands the fine line between acquiescing to what is not proper and establishing what is right as a rule.

Many superintendents suggest that school board member turnover is a major factor in not only how effective they can be in their job, but whether they can survive (Johnson, 1996). School board members are not remaining on boards for as long as they used to. It is not even unusual for most of the board to turn over in three or four years. These frequent changes in board makeup create problems for the superintendent (Hayes, 2001). It's almost like starting over. Initiatives that were important one month earlier may be abandoned, and the spirit of cooperation sometimes deteriorates. New school board members may mistreat the superintendent and even view him or her as an adversary, especially if they campaigned on a mandate to "straighten out" or "get rid of" the person who is leading the district.

One crucial strategy in creating a solid relationship with new board members is for the superintendent to establish an effective new school board member orientation program (Danzberger, 1998). A formal program for bringing newcomers to the board up to speed is an important way that a superintendent can help prevent the confusion and frustration that can damage a board partnership (Houston & Eadie, 2002). A uniform, high-quality orientation program can also transcend some of the preelection rhetoric and prepare board members for potential board conflict. A key here is consistency; the superintendent should not tailor an orientation program to fit an errant, new school board member. Such a strategy will backfire if it is felt that it was a planned scheme. Treat all board members with fairness and consistency, and respect will likely follow.

Providing board members with the knowledge they need is especially important for superintendents today, and the superintendent should be personally involved in training for each new member (Hayes, 2001). District policy making has become more complex, and there are greater expectations of board members. Even members who are informed about issues may lack experience in areas related to technology, curriculum evaluation, or collective bargaining. While many school board associations conduct training sessions for new board members, orientation is often left to the superintendent and other board members. According to the 10-year AASA survey of superintendents in 2000, almost half of the superintendents polled indicated they provide board members with their primary orientation (Glass, 2000d). During the orientation it is essential to emphasize the specific roles of both board members and the superintendent, and include an explanation of the laws regarding open and closed meetings. It is also a good idea for board members to attend conferences and meetings to continue to learn about current education topics (Hayes, 2001).

One of the superintendent's primary responsibilities as CEO of the district is to build and maintain strategically significant relationships (Houston & Eadie, 2002). The most challenging relationship that a superintendent will work to develop is probably with the school board (Hayes, 2001). It is also the most critical. More than any other factor, how productively and harmoniously the superintendent-school board partnership structure works will determine the quality of leadership in the district, and significantly impacts the success of the entire educational enterprise (Houston & Eadie, 2002). Therefore it is crucial for the superintendent to build a positive and long-term partnership with board members (Eadie, 2003) and put maintaining the relationship at the top of the list (Houston & Eadie, 2002). That relationship remains a key factor in not only the superintendent's continued employment, but his or her success (Glass, 2000d), for little can be accomplished without the board's support. Only by working together can the board and the superintendent create the kind of foundation that is needed to allow the superintendent to effectively administer district policies and lead operations (Carter & Cunningham, 1997).

5
Internal and External Relations

It cannot be assumed that a superintendent comes equipped with all the tools necessary to master the complex skills needed to relate to all of the publics in public education. Note the description of who is being discussed here—*publics*, which is plural. There is more than one public. As a result, how a superintendent handles the leadership responsibility of developing and maintaining relationships with the various publics within the school district can make the difference between success and failure. Although the superintendent spends most of his or her time with the school board and other district administrators, it is still important to realize that the superintendent's ultimate success depends on maintaining a satisfactory level of trust and support from various stakeholders in the district (Hayes, 2001).

The demands and expectations that the publics have for schools are many and often conflicting. It is also apparent that schools must answer to a return of interest in a broad-based type of school administration and decision making that ensures multiple and diverse concerns are served (Brunner & Björk, 2001). But because communities differ appreciably in terms of their involvement in political activity and support for public education, there is no one formula that is effective for building and maintaining community support. Wise superintendents develop their own plans that are best suited to the community and the needs of their own school district, keeping in mind both educational and community values (Kowalski, 1999).

As the school leader, the superintendent must understand that his or her role is not to simply respond to public demands, but to proactively listen and develop responses through structured programs and strategies that best serve the school community. One part of that leadership in school-community relations centers on determining what needs to be communicated to the many publics (Kowalski, 1999). The superintendent's ability to communicate effectively with all groups within the school system and within the larger community will help clarify issues, erase concerns, and articulate direction. If the superintendent can communicate through action that the focus should always be on students—while building bridges among school staff, parents, and community—success is more likely to follow.

This chapter will delineate the internal and external publics and suggest effective leadership strategies to deal with them. One is not more important than the others, however giving attention to one at the expense of another is a road map to disaster. While there will appear to be some demarcation between internal and external publics in this discussion, it is important to note that persons internal to an organization may also have an external role. For example, it is generally understood that district employees are an internal public. But if those employees live within the taxing jurisdiction of the school district, they are taxpayers as well, and part of the external public as taxpayers. They may see issues that interest them as employees in a new light when they also consider their role as taxpayers.

The internal public generally includes school board members, central office administrators, building administrators, teachers, noncertified support staff, and service providers such as attorneys and auditors. Each has a stake in the school system based upon the unique nature of their position. School board members, for example, as mentioned in preceding chapters, have authority only when they sit as a corporate body at a duly constituted meeting. Again, this means that outside of the meeting, a member of the board has no authority (Sharp & Walter, 2004). The question often arises as to whether outside of a meeting a school board member is part of the external public. The technical answer is yes. A person on the school board is a member of the lay public when not officially sitting with a legal quorum of the board at a duly constituted meeting.

Yet as often cited by savvy superintendents when advising their boards on behavior away from a constituted meeting, a school board member can never step out of his or her role. A school board member cannot take one hat off and put on another depending on the situation. Practically speaking, school board members serve in a role where the judging public sets the rules for how they are viewed. They are generally seen as board members, whether they are at the board table or in the community.

While the public and some of the staff may have difficulty with the line between a board member as an official or as a citizen, the superintendent should remain very clear on how board members should be treated. If the superintendent develops and maintains the proper relationship with school board members, they will likely respond in a positive manner in turn. Although it is helpful to get to know members of the board (Hayes, 2001), veteran superintendents have advised against personal associations, or keeping them to a minimum because there of the potential for conflict and politics, a loss of objectivity, or expecting personal favors (Kowalski, 1999).

As stated earlier, the superintendent is obligated to always deliver timely and accurate communication to the school board at all times. After all, board members are the ultimate volunteers. They deserve respect, and they should be kept in the communication loop as a matter of course. Whether it is acknowledged or not, school board members serve as liaisons between the public and the school district (Sharp & Walter, 2004). They routinely hear information that the public will not ordinarily tell district employees. In the best case scenario, school board members will listen to the external public voices and direct the issues back through the system by passing the information on to the superintendent. In an American Association of School Administrators survey of superintendents in 2000, more than 90 percent of the superintendents reported that they considered board members to be a powerful source of information (Glass, 2000d).

It is typically assumed by the casual observer that administrators both at the central office and building levels are in situations where they know all there is to know about the district. While such an assumption is generally unrealistic, it is prudent for the superintendent to be aware of this public view. According to superintendents, they also place significant weight on the information they obtain from the central office staff (Glass, 1992). Care must be taken not to take for granted the support and understanding of administrative staff, which will only occur when the superintendent makes it a priority to establish adequate communication links with administrators. Like the superintendent's relationship with the school board, the superintendent's ability to work with and lead faculty and staff is essential for the success of the administration (Hayes, 2001).

Depending on the size of the district, communication may be handled in a variety of ways. In a large district where there is a sizeable central office, the superintendent should set up structures where he or she can have meaningful interface with all central office administrators. To do so establishes a culture of communication for the district and builds in a feedback mechanism so that the superintendent can stay apprised on issues that occur within and outside the school system on a consistent basis. School site administrators, on the other hand, often feel isolated from the district due to lack of proximity to the action. The superintendent should see to it that school site administrators feel a sense of ownership to the big picture, and not just to their individual buildings. The superintendent should also lead the effort to recognize the value of site administrators. An appropriate first step is to get to know who they are and address them by name. Another strategy is to establish regular meetings with the site administrators so that they have their own audience with the superintendent, unfiltered by central office administrators. However the meetings are structured, the key is to establish consistent and reliable forums for site administrators to interact with the superintendent.

A good way for the superintendent, as well as central office administrators, to enhance communication with subordinates on the part of the superintendent is to find ways to show site level administrators that they are appreciated for their contributions. Noticing when they engage in activities that bring positive regard to the school system and sending notes of appreciation at such times is one way for the recipient to know that those in authority with the school system are paying attention and care. Administrators can also be applauded for their first-rate work at public board meetings (Hayes, 2001). Showing respect for administrative staff by involving them in meaningful discussions, recognizing their efforts, and investing in them as valued team members will go a long way toward fostering the team relationship that is so vital to the success of the superintendent, and by extension, the entire school system.

It is said that in so many ways the teaching staff forms the backbone of the school system. Without competent teaching, there is no education, and the school district will ultimately fail. If schools are about students, then the teachers are indeed the most important of the internal publics. Teachers in this context—as generally understood by the lay public—include librarians, counselors, diagnosticians, nurses, and therapists, as well as itinerant teachers and teacher aides. By virtue of direct contact with students and parents, they have the unique opportunity to influence how the external publics perceive the quality of the education system. Many, if not most members of the lay public, also judge a school system based on how it relates to its teachers. This internal public is the core, the centerpost for actual learning in the system, and must absolutely be kept informed and involved in district affairs. As with administrative staff, teachers must be respected, encouraged, shown appreciation, and recognized for their important role in the system.

In some school districts it may be somewhat problematic for the administration to formally recognize teachers due to union politics that only allow communication through union leadership. Obviously this poses a unique challenge, but does not lessen the superintendent's responsibility to establish a solid relationship with teachers, through whatever mechanism is available. To do otherwise would only be detrimental, as a positive relationship with this group enables the district to function much more effectively.

Therefore, it is foolish not to appropriately support and involve teachers in all aspects of the school system. Working closely with teachers and making them feel that they are a part of the team is absolutely essential to the success of the superintendent and other administrators.

When a new superintendent secures the confidence of teachers and expresses the same confidence in them, teachers tend to take a broader view of their work and show more interest in district initiatives (Johnson, 1996). Low district performance will, after all, end up on the shoulders of the superintendent, who is the leader. Whether or not the superintendent is directly responsible for poor educational instruction is beside the point. Understandably, as CEO, the superintendent is accountable for the entire school district's performance—educationally, financially, administratively (Eadie, 2003)—and that's how it will be viewed by the external publics.

Secretaries have long been viewed by school leaders as the front line soldiers. Using the battlefield analogy, this group of employees is the first to make contact both inside and outside of the system, and the impression they create is important (Hayes, 2001; Sharp & Walter, 2004). They tend not to be on the inside of high-level discussions as are administrators, and they certainly are not the center of the instructional process as are teachers, however in many instances they are the first to know about serious matters that affect the district or school sites. They are often the first person that a member of the external public may encounter when telephoning or visiting a school or the district office. Acknowledging these facts requires that the prudent superintendent or administrator keep the secretarial staff informed and in the loop about issues regarding the district or school. Holding a forum for this group, chaired by the superintendent and allowing for discussion and feedback, is imperative to running a good school system. An astute administrator will establish a professional rapport with secretaries to test ideas and proposals, and consider viewpoints that might otherwise have been dismissed.

Loyal secretaries can contribute to a superintendent's success. A point that is sometimes overlooked is the trust that must be placed in them (Hayes, 2001). Secretaries produce communication documents on a daily basis. They are routinely privileged to sensitive and confidential information. They are trusted to represent the administration and the district by their decorum and deportment. Thus, special care should be taken when selecting a secretary. While often viewed as servants, secretaries must possess great intellectual skills, not unlike their administrative bosses. They are indeed gatekeepers and clearinghouses for information. Savvy administrators will make certain secretaries know they are valuable to the organization, and will stress their importance to the team. Proper procedures should be established that show appreciation for the work secretaries do and recognize the valuable service they provide for the entire school system.

Noncertified support staff, similar to the secretarial staff, reinforces the mission of the school district and school sites. While this group is often easily overlooked, most school systems would face certain disaster if the support staff was not present. Like secretaries, this class of employee is likely to be the first that a visitor will encounter. For example, a citizen entering a school building may be greeted by a custodian. The value of a capable custodian is further amplified by the appearance of the building. A visitor will frequently carry away impressions of the district or a school site based simply on a building's cleanliness. Just as with a person, the appearance of a building or the grounds implies whether or not there is a sense of care and concern. Similar judgments are made as citizens view the work and behavior of cafeteria workers. Bus drivers comprise yet another group that gives an impression of the district as they pick up and deliver children to and from their destinations. Whatever roles support staff play in school districts, they are important to the organization. Good relations with the external public to a large extent depend on good relations with the district staff. Although the superintendent may have minimal direct contact, the staff's contact with the external public is immense (Sharp & Walter, 2004), and that includes support staff. Like any other staff, support staff members have contacts outside the school system who are influenced by opinions and make judgments based on positive or negative reports about a school district. A superintendent who realizes the need to recognize employees for the valuable service they perform will not overlook support staff members since this class of employee has evolved to become a crucial part of the overall effectiveness of a school system.

Internal communication is essential to the success of a superintendent and other school administrators. Employees who feel trusted and supported by central office leaders will be more willing to take part in plans for school improvement (Carter & Cunningham, 1997). Communication with employees occurs both formally and informally. While informal communication will happen without a plan, it is vital that communication within the school system is also formally structured and not left to chance. Formal communication plans are essential to successful administration and will serve to put informal communication in perspective. For example, if something egregious occurs at a school site, the informal communication network, or "grapevine," will immediately send out several versions of the incident. However a proper, formal plan will appropriately communicate what really happened to the internal publics so that the informal version will be overshadowed. When the formal process is consistent, the informal will be less active. If internal publics are valued and engaged, they will also assist in promoting positive communications, as well as monitoring and influencing the behavior of their fellow employees.

There are various methods, strategies, and tools that can be utilized for internal communication. Skill and consistency determine the effectiveness of the communication much more than the approach that is chosen. Examples are: newsletters, voice mail, memos, e-mail, meetings, briefings;

and debriefings. Such traditional communication devices have their place and must be utilized, however enlightened leaders will establish structures that foster two-way communication with an opportunity for feedback. Whichever mechanism is used, it is important to have a formal structure in place that is flexible enough to adjust when members of the internal public offer sound advice. If the superintendent does not gain credibility with district employees, he or she will never have credibility with the community either (Owen & Ovando, 2000).

External publics are not as easily defined as the previously discussed internal publics. We could sum up the discussion of the external publics by simply stating that external publics encompass everyone. Obviously the subject is far more complex. One common thought is that external publics are outsiders to the school system. On the contrary, the reason this topic is important is because of the interest that the external publics have in the school system. The external publics tend to be voices that want to be heard. They tend to be players on the sidelines who want to get in the game. One way to look at the external publics and who they really are is to consider them as groups, just as we did the internal publics. In such delineation, external publics will have far more component groups than will the internal publics. Even with the understanding that a vast number of groups can be identified, there is the risk that some groups will invariably be overlooked.

A skilled superintendent will understand the need to identify the external forces and groups that relate to the school district, and the superintendent's commitment to include these groups must be genuine. Anything short of true sensitivity to community involvement will be quickly dismissed as pejorative and patronizing. Depending on the school system, the external publics will take on different faces. Size, complexity, and diversity of the population all come into play when determining how external communication and involvement are handled. The insightful superintendent will get to know the community and work to install an external communications plan that will offer the greatest chance for success. Superintendents and school boards that are able to maintain a high standard of credibility realize the importance of involving large numbers of citizens. They understand that the chances of passing referenda will be enhanced if a majority of the community holds a positive opinion of the district (Hoyle, et al., 2005).

School superintendents must be keenly aware of the range of interests and belief systems within the community to gain the broad-based support that is necessary to maintain a high-performing school system. A wide range of interests on the part of citizens in a school district suggests diverse constituent groups. Such diversity begs the question of how the district can please everyone. Certainly, it is not an easy task. The first step is to understand the nature of the social forces within in the community. Because school systems are so different in their constituent makeup, no attempt will be made to formally name organizations or distinct groups. Rather we will concentrate on the responsibility to recognize that organizations and groups represent a spectrum of attitudes and orientations. All organizations demand loyalty from their members, and depending on the issue, may oppose certain school policies and procedures, and take positions that are inconsistent with the best work of the administration and the board.

The best case scenario is for the superintendent to identify every single organization and formal group within the school district and write an introductory letter to them inviting their involvement. Such a letter should not be one that invites them to a meeting at the central office headquarters to "hear" the administration, but rather a request to allow the superintendent to appear before the group on its turf. This approach may produce some shock, but most groups will be pleased. Thus, the superintendent must be prepared to spend several months moving from organization to organization and from group to group. These groups may be civic organizations, gardening clubs, ethnic groups, neighborhood associations, clergy, Realtors, senior citizen groups, business associations, and so on. The key to the visits is to uphold a theme of neutrality and openness. Even if these groups are apolitical or unwilling to take public stances on issues related to schools, there will surely be individuals within the groups who will be influenced by the district's approach. Obviously the superintendent has to be prepared to receive some harsh criticism directed at the system. While not a simple assignment, this "take it to the people" strategy will pay big dividends. The superintendent needs to keep in mind that a public school system is the public's business, and as such, the public has the right to ask tough questions.

Another important step to take while completing the round of external visits is a follow-up letter of appreciation with a promise to contact the group again in the near future. Once all of the visits are concluded, the next written contact should express the district's desire to establish an ongoing relationship with the group. Given the fact that most groups are large, and there are many groups, a suitable technique would be to request that each group select a key communicator to join other group representatives in regular forums with the superintendent to talk about the school district. Then each key communicator will take information back to his or her group as well as report on contributions made at the forum on the group's behalf. Moreover, the individuals in the key communicator peer group will be the ones who the superintendent will contact to ensure that the various groups receive public information of interest on a timely basis.

Again, a major reason for identifying these special interest groups and bringing them into the fold is because they are not likely to be involved with the traditional structures typically found in school districts. The parent-teacher association and the district citizens advisory committee tend to be the groups that are most visible in many school districts. While serving a very worthwhile purpose, these traditional structures are often viewed as insider clubs or school system clones, and discourage the involvement of those who may want to offer another opinion.

Before summarizing this section, we need to discuss a group that was not included as one of the external publics. That group is the media, which seems to have so much influence on school systems that it deserves special mention. While the word *media* is plural, it is used to refer to any of the various mediums—newspaper, radio, or television. Most school districts regard the local newspaper as the primary news vehicle, rather than the electronic media of radio and television. And school officials generally have guarded responses to media inquiries, based on their experience that most news about school districts is negative. According to a recent survey, 55 percent of both superintendents and principals report that problems with media coverage are increasing. In large districts, the numbers are even worse, with 60 percent reporting uninformed or sensational coverage, a concentration on bad news, and mistakes among the complaints (Farkas, et al., 2003).

The media, however, do not have to be enemies of the school district (Hayes, 2001). It is far more sensible to become their partners. District leaders should be ready to build and maintain effective media relationships, and instead of restricting information, they should look at the media as valuable resources for exchanging information (Kowalski, 1999). School superintendents and other administrators need to recognize that there are effective and skillful ways to work with the media. It is not a given that reporters are negative news junkies who set out to destroy the school district. Their job is to report factual stories as assigned and maintain the relationships necessary to carry out their duties. Yet some administrators mistakenly expect reporters to perform as public relation advocates for the schools. As a result, there is often tension between the news media and the school districts.

The best time to establish constructive relationships with the media is before a crisis occurs. As with special interest groups, the superintendent should seek out the heads of the local media outlets and set up meetings just to talk. During those meetings, the superintendent should describe what he or she believes a relationship between the school district and the media should entail. A commitment should be made to employ effective management and leadership practices to ensure that a clear, concise vision for the school district is communicated. The superintendent should personally pledge to work with district staff and employees to promote the importance of a balanced relationship with the media and promise to be proactive in revealing information to them, as opposed to stonewalling and making them dig for stories. All school district representatives should also provide accurate information to the media when they are called upon to do so. The superintendent can act as a role model and set the tone for appropriate media interaction (Kowalski, 1999).

In addition to making a commitment to cooperate and build relationships with media bosses, the superintendent should not neglect the importance of good communication with local reporters. Reporters are professionals and need to be treated that way. Respecting their position and assisting them in doing their work is a smart move (Hayes, 2001). Formal meetings should be held with reporters on a regular and consistent basis as well, being mindful that reporters work against deadlines and production schedules (Kowalski, 1999). Regular meetings will serve the needs of both parties as they relate to the timeliness of disseminating information. They will also enable the superintendent and district staff to get to know the reporters as people and erase the idea of them being enemies.

Other alliance building strategies include inviting the media to school events and providing them with free passes to attend district activities. Reporters will also appreciate being complimented for a well-written story about the district, as they don't often receive positive feedback (Hayes, 2001). Making members of the media feel special will go a long way toward cementing sound relationships. The more reporters know about school administrators and the jobs they perform, the more apt they are to respect them. Sustained relationship building with all levels of the media is likely to result in greater fairness and objectivity when they report on district events.

Proficient internal and external relations are vital to a school district. As the leader, the superintendent needs to be skillful and understand the value of continually seeking methods to improve connections with all of the district's publics, and involve them in more meaningful ways. A well-founded public relations program must be planned and not left to chance. The superintendent must take charge of the effort for the school system in order to maximize the opportunity for success. This leadership responsibility is so crucial that it cannot be delegated or assigned to a public relations office.

While some districts, due to their size, may have a public relations officer, this person cannot be a substitute for the direct involvement of the superintendent when it comes to interacting with internal and external publics. No matter how skilled the public relations professional, he or she is at best an ombudsman and someone who would possibly lack the superintendent's personal touch and perspective of the community. But, this person should serve as a key advisor to the superintendent. If a public relations specialist is employed by the school district, it would also be wise for that person to be included in the superintendent's cabinet and interact with other top level administrators on a regular basis.

Mastering the art of dealing effectively with the various publics can often make the difference between success and failure of a school superintendent. Public schools must have the support of both those who work for the school district and the community which they serve (Norton, et al., 1996). In working to bring about change, a superintendent needs to establish reliable lines of communication with everyone who wants to have a voice in setting school policy. Relationship building is time-consuming, but essential (Hayes, 2001). Communication may be the most crucial skill of the superintendency, especially when it comes to interacting with the external public (Hoyle, et al., 2005) because today there are greater expectations that superintendents will maintain continuing dialogue with the wider community (Kowalski, 1999). Therefore superintendents should carefully evaluate the information needs of the district staff and each interest group in the community, and then develop a system of strategies to convey that information by the most efficient means (Hoyle, et al., 2005).

6

Government Relations

It could be argued that government cannot be separated from politics, yet government relations is of sufficient import to be treated as a subject unto itself. This chapter will discuss the topic of government relations, while political savvy will be covered elsewhere. The astute superintendent will clearly see the need for developing and maintaining an expertise in both.

The question of how school districts relate to other government jurisdictions is a significant subject that superintendents need to understand in order to enhance their chances for success. Superintendents must also try to keep up-to-date on issues that affect the school district at all levels of government (Hayes, 2001). For the purpose of this discussion, the *government* in government relations is defined as the local, state, and federal governments. To further clarify, a local government may be a village, a town, or a city. Every school district in the country is situated within government jurisdictions besides the jurisdiction of the school district itself. In some cases, the school district and another governmental entity are one in the same. However the most common model is where the school district is independent, and by proximity is associated with other governmental jurisdictions or municipalities, meaning the school district crosses over more than one town's boundaries. In either case, the school district is likely to be independent from any one of those jurisdictions in which it sits. The distinction and division from the local government may be clear to the municipality and the school district, but many citizens do not necessarily see the independence. Even when citizens understand the demarcation, they often reject the notion that the two should be independent.

What distinguishes a school district from a municipality is generally based on at least three factors. First, it is a governmental entity with its own taxing authority; it is not tied to any other jurisdiction for receipt of taxpayer funds. Next, a school district has its own school board that is independent from boards or councils in other local governments. Also, most school districts are responsible for their own budgets and are not required to submit them for review or approval to any other governmental body. However, like other governmental bodies, a school district is accountable for its budget to the public, and by extension, to other governmental jurisdictions that overlap its boundaries. To maintain their separate identities, a school district generally does not share leadership or employees with other governments. Yet there are some exceptions. Joint agreements, for example, allow for sharing land and/or facilities. Otherwise a school district is usually strictly an independent, legal entity and has no obligation to other governments.

Some might suggest that superintendents of schools have enough to do and do not need to be poking around in other governmental entities. Such a narrow view of a superintendent's responsibility is seriously misguided. It simply makes good sense for a school district to maintain positive relationships with municipalities, and a school district that would adopt the idea that it does not have to consider the governments around it is shortsighted. While it may seem that the advantages of maintaining solid relationships with local municipalities would be apparent, this is not so, in light of the fact that most publics and even members of the school board do not realize the necessity. Thus, the superintendent must be the one catalyst to make sure that all concerned understand the importance of government relations. Should all or some members of a school board hold the opinion that a school district should go it alone and isolate itself from local governments, it's up to the superintendent to take the lead in changing their attitude. The job of building and maintaining government relationships often falls on the school superintendent more so than individual board members. Remember, individual members of the board have no legal standing outside the corporate body at a duly constituted board meeting. As a rule, school boards and municipal councils do not hold joint meetings either. Given this consideration, it makes it even more important that the superintendent—as the chief executive officer of the school board—is the person who makes sure that local government relations are maintained.

In one school system where the district touched all or parts of 11 municipalities, the school superintendent scheduled annual meetings with each of the municipal mayors. The meetings were held to maintain relationships instead of waiting for a situation to occur before the leaders met. When two or more jurisdictions share adjoining territory, there will likely be a specific reason to meet from time to time. However with no special purpose, routine annual visits will pave the way for future meetings with neighboring or overlapping governments when there are issues that force them to the table. Whether the school district shares territory with one or more governmental jurisdictions, it is easier to develop and maintain a cordial relationship with local elected officials than it is to have to start one in a hurry. A school superintendent may also find it useful to develop relationships with the various city, town, or village managers. While managers are administrators and not elected officials—just like the school superintendent—they do have influence with their elected bosses.

Another technique for maintaining good relations with neighboring or overlapping governments is to assign school district representatives to attend the board or council meetings (Hayes, 2001). In turn, neighboring governments will often send a representative to sit in on school board meetings. It would be viewed as a positive gesture on the part of the school board president or superintendent to acknowledge the presence of the assigned representatives from neighboring governments when they are visitors at school board meetings. Invitations to school activities also let government officials know that they are held in high regard. To help them understand the sincerity of the invitation, a school district may consider investing in free passes to school activities for municipal government officials.

Again, recognizing their presence when they appear at functions is an excellent way to show them that they are appreciated. Coexisting harmoniously with neighboring municipalities and having positive structures in place to maintain good relations would seem to be a given. In some cases the need may be obvious, but the understanding of how to make it happen may be lacking. The point is not whether the techniques suggested here will work in particular school districts, but rather that school districts should find methods that will work for them in developing and maintaining solid relationships with neighboring governments.

Superintendents and board members also need to be informed about and take part in what is happening at the state and federal levels regarding public education. Although some states are more involved than others, all state governments pass legislation and regulations that affect instruction, and now more often, assessment (Hayes, 2001). Moving from the local level to state level government, relationships are still important, but the approach will be different. Working with state government tends to take on the appearance of political involvement more so than with local governments, and clearly any involvement by the superintendent or other school officials may be labeled as such. The purpose of this discussion is not to view the superintendent or other school officials as political players, but as good communicators who establish a high profile with certain state officials so that the district is viewed in the best possible light.

Every state, by constitution, statute, and practice generally assumes that the education of public school students is a primary function and an integral part of the state's organizational structure (Hoyle, et al., 2005). Such notions have been tested from time to time in the state and federal courts and have been supported. Therefore, each state in the United States is legally responsible for supporting and maintaining the public schools within its borders. Given this responsibility, state legislation typically establishes a state education agency, which usually consists of a state board of education led by a chief state school officer, and a state department of education.

Depending on the state, members of the state board of education may be elected or appointed by the state legislature or the governor, and their actions are controlled by the legislatures (Kowalski, 2001). The chief state school officer can be called the state superintendent, the commissioner of education, or the secretary of education, again, depending on the state. The state enacts legislation related to education, determines school tax rates, and allots financial aid to local school districts. State boards of education are separate from the state legislature, but they serve an important advisory function regarding policy and education statutes (Kowalski, 2001). Through a state education agency, the state is usually involved in setting standards for certification, training, and in some cases, the actual curriculum. Some states even set minimum salaries for personnel. To one degree or another, states also are involved in providing special services such as transportation and selecting appropriate textbooks.

Most states have a school code, which is a collection of all the laws that govern education in the state. This code is the guidebook for schools operating in the state. State statutes are typically divided into two groups. The first is mandatory laws that require school districts to adhere to specific rules or criteria for programs or functions. The second group covers permissive laws that define the functions that are delegated to the school districts under specific conditions. Local school boards are considered creations of the state and are given the authority to run local school systems.

Within recent years, state legislatures and education agencies, along with local school boards across the country, have taken a more active role in education reforms. It is therefore helpful for superintendents to communicate with elected local state officials (Hayes, 2001). Obviously, one motive to do so is to have some advantage when education issues come up for a vote. To facilitate a relationship with elected state officials, the superintendent needs to become familiar with whom they are. Depending on state structure, the representatives may be members of the House of Representatives and/or state senators. The superintendent, especially when new to the position, needs to contact each of the officials by phone, introduce himself or herself, and request a one-on-one visit.

State officials are usually busy people who may not be available as soon as desired, but persistence should eventually result in an appointment. Besides making this a "get acquainted" meeting, the superintendent should spend the majority of the time listening. Elected state officials generally have a lot to say and often enjoy the flattery of having the floor. Of course if the state official asks questions, the superintendent should be prepared to answer. However, the superintendent should be careful not to be demanding at this juncture. At the conclusion of the meeting, the superintendent should inquire about the contact process for talking with the state official in the future. If the ideal relationships do not materialize right away, the superintendent should continue to occasionally call the various officials until they become comfortable enough to reciprocate.

An important step that superintendents and local school boards need to take with state legislators is developing legislative positions on various bills that affect education. This process should be done in public so that the news media will notice the importance that the board places on pending legislation. The state officials will also be aware that the board is discussing important legislative issues prior to them receiving any documents. When the official document is complete, a copy should be mailed to each legislator to solicit their support for the positions established by the board and superintendent. Many superintendents maintain close ties with their local state legislators and, along with their administrative staffs, try to influence decisions in state government. Sometimes superintendents can also build a relationship that encourages legislators to contact them about proposed legislation (Hayes, 2001). It should be made clear that direct calls from the state official to the superintendent would be welcomed and even expected if the superintendent could lend assistance.

Before the legislative session gets underway, the school board and superintendent should sponsor a public legislative forum wherein the elected state officials are invited to sit on a panel and explain their positions on various education issues, as well as respond to questions. The school district should assemble a panel of citizen participants in addition to the school board itself. The panel could include key communicators or representatives of citizens committees, depending on the number of participants the board desires. State legislators will generally appreciate the opportunity to appear in public as a way of demonstrating their responsiveness to constituents. And once the forum is established as an annual event, state legislators may very well look forward to the meeting as a part of their involvement with the school community.

The superintendent, as the individual who represents the school district in most important issues, should also be available to travel to the state capital when the legislature is in session and give testimony as often as issues require. Beyond that, the superintendent should attend legislative sessions when testimony is not required. Such visibility can show that the superintendent supports the legislators who represent the school community. At a point early in the legislative session, a trip to the state capital should be planned for members of the school board and select citizens. The event could be billed as a "lobby day" for the school district. This activity makes two important points: 1.) The school district understands the importance of citizen involvement in the legislative process and is willing to invest in a daylong trip to demonstrate the seriousness of the commitment; and 2.) The school district's presence at the state capital gives positive recognition to the legislators who represent the school community. These legislators will appreciate the effort on the part of the school district to support them with their presence rather than just lip service.

Although positive relationships should be established between school officials and state legislators, it should be cautioned that both parties need to understand the wisdom of neutrality when it comes to school officials being involved in a legislator's election or reelection campaign. This may prove difficult for some school board members who tend to bond with certain legislators and may be tempted to show overt support. The danger in campaigning for individuals is that if a supported candidate loses, it may be difficult for the school board to establish the desired relationship with the challenger who successfully unseated the incumbent. Wounds may be so deep that the district may never enjoy the positive regard of the new legislator during his or her term in office. While it may be tempting for school board members, the superintendent absolutely should never take part in the politics of an election at any level. To do so could cause serious damage to the superintendent's credibility.

Historically, public school boards and superintendents have been primarily involved with local and state governments. However, during the latter part of the 20th century, the federal government started taking on a greater role in the governance of local districts (Hayes, 2001), more heavily influencing education through federal funding and its accompanying regulations. This situation is requiring further involvement by school boards and superintendents in the processes where education decisions are made (Carter & Cunningham, 1997), at the federal level. A recent example of those federal regulations is the revision of the landmark Elementary and Secondary Education Act first passed in 1965 and now called the No Child Left Behind (NCLB) Act of 2001. This federal legislation has been referred to as the most intrusive effort by the federal government to influence education policy and practice.

NCLB incorporates significant regulations for evaluating the level of instruction in America's schools in such a way that the quality of individual schools can be determined (Popham, 2004). State accountability systems, testing programs, and rules and regulations mandating standards for teachers are among the requirements that states must meet. Students in grades three through eight must take annual standards-based tests, the results of which can be used to compare schools and school districts. School sites, more so than school districts, are monitored for "adequate progress." Schools or districts that do not achieve adequate progress for two consecutive years will be held accountable, and states will be forced to take corrective measures which range from financing student tutoring to paying for students to transfer to another school (Harvey, 2005c). Also, states must ensure that all teachers of core academic subjects are "highly qualified" by 2005-2006. States and districts are required to prepare performance report cards for the community that include information about teacher qualifications and the number of classes taught by teachers who do not have the "highly qualified" label.

Many school districts, school boards, and superintendents are still trying to figure out how to appropriately implement the NCLB legislation. This is serious legislation that is not likely to disappear even if the political party in power changes. The law, after all, was drafted by a bipartisan panel of federal legislators, which gives it stature to transcend party politics. The superintendents of local school districts are obligated to be very familiar with the law and all of its implementation components. Because the superintendent is the chief spokesperson for the school district (Hayes, 2001), he or she must always be prepared to explain federal legislation that relates to public education. Not only must the superintendent be able to articulate federal positions with the public, but to the staff as well. The staff, as a matter of practice, usually takes its cues from the behavior of the superintendent. Thus, the superintendent needs to be careful not to unduly criticize federal laws and regulations, while at the same time understanding the responsibility to provide input that can improve public education where the law allows.

The school board and the superintendent also must be mindful of court decisions, such as those concerned with racial segregation in schools. Depending on the school district and its demographics, the superintendent and board have an obligation to "toe the line" with regard to following court mandates. This duty includes responding to all of the requirements relating to students who fall under Public Law 94-142, which is legislation that mandates nondiscrimination of handicapped and special needs students, and Section 504 of the Rehabilitation Act (part of the Americans with Disabilities Act), which requires that all facilities in a school district be accessible to the physically disabled. Obviously there are many more federal laws that affect school systems that must be observed. As such, the superintendent is expected to be knowledgeable about them all and advise the school board of the district's responsibility.

Much like the need for the superintendent and school board to know their state legislators, it's a good idea to establish ties with federal legislators. But a close relationship is not likely. Unlike state officials, federal legislators are less willing to spend personal time with an individual local school board. That is not to say it is impossible, and a special effort should be made to create relationships with key federal staff members. However education in the United States is considered a state and/or local government function and not a federal responsibility. There are 50 different state systems, with many variations in how local school systems are administered within each state. All together there are approximately 15,000 local school districts, each with their own rules within the bounds of state law. Again, although the Constitution of the United States makes no mention of public education, the Tenth Amendment reserves to the states all powers not specifically delegated to the federal government or prohibited by the Constitution. This is the amendment that provides the basis for states accepting primary legal authority for public education. Yet states have made it a common practice to delegate the responsibility for the day-to-day operations of public schools to local school districts.

Most local school districts do not have the resources to go it alone when attempting to influence federal or state legislation. But there are many national and state educational interest groups that purport to speak for or critique public education on a regular basis. There is wisdom and value in the superintendent and school board learning who those power brokers are, and trying to influence their platform. Success with such groups is more likely when several school districts combine forces to communicate local positions. In addition, reaching out beyond the local politicians can often bring attention to them in the form of added publicity, just when they may be seeking support for important issues affecting school districts within their jurisdiction.

Superintendents—whether they like it or not—are being pulled into discussions involving federal governance of their school districts. The movement to set national curriculum standards is changing the way school districts across the country operate. Other than district finances, the greatest pressure superintendents face is related to achieving higher student performance on standards-based tests (Hoyle, et al., 2005). Regular student assessments are designed to keep a district moving toward the standards, however the demands for accountability are taking the decisions about district goals far from the classroom, with federal laws dictating what states must do to receive federal funding. The states, of course, then pass those same demands on to local school districts (Cambron-McCabe & Harvey, 2005). Although many factors may contribute to low test scores, without improvement, the superintendent will eventually be called to task. In some districts, those test results serve as the primary benchmark a school board will use to judge the success of its superintendent (Hayes, 2001).

The debate over the federal government's role in public education is likely to continue. But the role of local school superintendents remains clear—to be strong advocates for public education and to stay within legal parameters when interpreting governmental issues to the public. That role includes creating relationships with local, state, and even federal politicians when it's in the best interest of the school district.

7

Fiscal Responsibility

A fiscally responsible superintendent has a full understanding of school district financing as it relates to such basics as where the revenue comes from and how budgets are developed to reflect the priorities of an array of district wants and demands. Yet it is possible to place fiscal responsibility on a number of players in the education system in addition to, or along with the superintendent. This chapter will touch upon all of those who are important to the financial health of a district and provide a clear picture of the superintendent's connection to the finance and budgeting process.

Public education systems do not enjoy the same flexibility as mainstream corporations that operate within the free enterprise system. With education systems, there is no sale of a traditional product or service to impact the bottom line. Public education systems across the country basically operate on appropriations, which in this context means the money comes from various forms of taxes. And when taxes are reduced, so is available funding for public education (Carter & Cunningham, 1997). In most school districts tax revenue comes from three basic sources. The largest is typically local property tax. State revenue, which is money paid by taxpayers throughout the state, comes in second. A lesser amount is provided by the federal government, usually through grants or targeted categorical funds. Although there are a number of other minor sources such as fees, sales, and gifts, they generally do not bring in enough revenue to make a difference in the budgeting process, and are often too insignificant to be considered reliable funding sources in a discussion about school finance.

Property taxes are those imposed on wealth in the form of tangible property. When most people think of tangible property, they think of real estate, but tangible property also consists of items such as machinery, equipment, vehicles, etc. Depending on the state, such tangible property can provide a significant portion of a school district's revenue. Some states also tax intangible property such as stocks, bonds, savings, and other investments. But there is no consistency across states in taxing tangible or intangible property. What does appear to be consistent, however, is how tangible real estate property is taxed. Real estate property comes in two forms: unimproved or improved. Unimproved real estate property is simply property or vacant land with no buildings or structures on it. Improved property, on the other hand, is land with a house, commercial building, or other structures. School districts generally levy ad valorem property taxes according to the value of the land and/or improvements.

The amount of equity that an owner or purchaser has in the property is not part of the equation in determining the tax bill. Property tax is assessed to the owner against the full value of the property even though a bank or mortgage holder may have the majority financial interest. Statutes that authorize local governments to levy taxes generally require an assessment of a property to determine its value. An appointed or elected official is usually responsible for placing a value on each taxable property in the school system. It is important for the superintendent of schools to understand the property tax process and be able to predict with a reasonable degree of accuracy just how much revenue property tax will yield from one year to the next, as well as from other state and federal appropriations (Hoyle, et al., 2005).

Another source of school district appropriations is money that comes by way of the state. Again, this is money that is primarily collected from taxpayers. States collect taxes in several ways. The most common, with the exception of about five states, is through income tax. These taxes are primarily levied against individuals who earn paychecks. State income tax is generally less complicated than federal income tax and is often a flat percentage for all wage earners irrespective of income level. Other taxes that states collect are sales tax, special use tax, gasoline tax, hotel/motel tax, etc. Regardless of the source, revenues coming to the state are deposited into a general fund and parceled out to the entities that the state is responsible for funding. Public schools, of course, are often one of the state's largest funding responsibilities.

It deserves mentioning that a debate continues regarding the best way to tax state residents for public services, including education. There is a school of thought that a state flat tax or proportional tax should replace property tax as the primary source for funding public schools. The argument against a proportional tax is that it is thought to be inequitable for all citizens. It seems that lower-and middle-class wage earners would end up being taxed mainly on basic living needs, while the upper middle-class would mainly be penalized for luxuries through this tax structure. On the other hand, the current reliance on property tax is considered regressive (Carter & Cunningham, 1997), since people can choose how much to pay for real estate. A multimillion dollar wage earner, for example, can control the amount of real estate taxes he pays by living in a house valued much lower than what his income can support, whereas under a flat tax applied to income, he would obviously pay more. The middle wage earner, however, is likely to be living in a house valued at several times more than his income and thus pays a disproportionate amount in property tax. The tax debate is likely to continue, with superintendents and school boards caught in the middle. District employees are demanding higher wages and more resources, middle income taxpayers are at their taxing limit, and the taxes of the wealthy are being progressively reduced. The end result for public education is very tight funding (Carter & Cunningham, 1997). And it appears that the power of the most wealthy to maintain the current system will likely make it difficult for meaningful tax reform to occur.

Occasionally there may be shortfalls in a district due to one or more sources of revenue failing to deliver the projected funds. Even in the best environment, where planning is precise and conservative, issues may arise over which the school system has no control. As a matter of fact, it is expected that such a situation will occur from time to time in most school districts. Most states have mechanisms built into their systems to handle these expected but unforeseen revenue dips. One mechanism employed by some states is the district's ability to provide a levy for the sole purpose of lending money to other funding categories that experience a temporary shortfall. This is a standby fund that operates like an internal bank. When education, operations, transportation, or other funds experience a shortfall, the special fund can be borrowed against to make up the difference and balance the budget. Law only allows it to be used as a bank for internal borrowing. Also under the law, when the first issues of taxes are collected by the school district, the special fund must be repaid. This is the legal method many school districts use to balance their budgets when there are manageable shortfalls that do not exceed the amount of money that they have in their internal bank. Even with this short-term solution, if the shortfall persists, the school district will have to reduce expenditures to align them with the adjusted revenue stream.

Another mechanism available to school districts when they have exhausted their ability to borrow internally is a loan from a bank. Banks are usually very willing to lend short-term money to school districts. The basis for the comfort that banks have in lending to school districts lies in the same rules that districts have for internal borrowing: They must repay the short-term loan back with the first issue of tax dollars to the school district. It is very safe for banks to loan money to school districts, and as a result, they tend to offer at a very favorable interest rate. These types of loans by banks to school districts are called Tax Anticipation Warrants. They are also sometimes referred to as Tax Anticipation Notes, depending on the bank. Schools and banks generally refer to these loans as TAWs or TANs. With either type, the school districts are required, as the description of the loan implies, to borrow against the anticipated amount of taxes to be received.

Laws in some states also allow school districts to move money from one funding source to another to shore up shortfalls. This is generally done by resolution of the school board during the course of the year, after the budget has been adopted. Again, like other types of borrowing, the lending source must be repaid when revenue is received from the taxing source. While all of the methods described here are legal, a school district must be very careful to not overextend its ability to return dollars to the lending sources as specified by law. To use these mechanisms, a school district must carefully monitor its financial position, even more so than in a normal fiscal environment.

A less popular and certainly more controversial of obtaining funds is a tax rate increase. When a school district reaches the point where the current tax rate does not produce the revenue needed to adequately fund the school district, basic decisions have to be made. The choices are simple: either revenue has to be increased, or expenditures have to be reduced. In most school systems it has to be demonstrated to the taxpaying public that the district has done all that it could to reduce expenditures before a tax rate increase can be requested. In some cases the public is very satisfied with the level of education that is being provided and is not willing to risk sacrificing quality for the sake of cutting the budget. In this instance, the public will vote for a tax rate increase in order not to lose ground.

Either way, school district officials must make the case for the additional revenue needed to fund the system. In some school systems across the country, the school board determines whether or not a tax rate increase is warranted. In those situations, the public does not get a vote. School boards that have this power "represent the public" and are responsible for making financial decisions on their behalf. If the public disagrees with a board's decision to raise taxes, there is a risk that board members will be voted out of office in the next election.

One trap that school districts need to avoid is the false security that comes from receiving gifts of money that may suffice for a short time, but do not represent a legitimate revenue stream that is needed to sustain ongoing expenses. There are stories about districts that relied on temporarily available "soft" money and found themselves in dire straits when it dried up. Even worse, districts that resort to fundraisers such as tag days, and other unreliable sources of funds, will quickly find themselves in trouble. When school districts get to the point that revenue from legitimate and reliable sources is no longer adequate, they absolutely must increase revenue or adjust expenditures to match incoming revenue.

Where the money comes from is obviously an important subject and one with which superintendents and boards must be thoroughly familiar. But let's shift from revenue to expenditures, which is the other side of the budgeting process. The expenditure side of the equation is just as important, yet sometimes receives a disproportionate amount of attention. How often have we heard that the school system needs to cut expenditures and everything will be fine? Of course it is not quite that simple. Obviously, fixed costs such as utilities, and supplies and equipment may not be controllable. In an effort to decrease spending, an attack is generally waged against salaries for personnel and facility maintenance. Too many people believe that you can merely cut the number of employees or their salaries and maintain the educational system just as well. It is also often suggested that adjustments can easily be made by trimming the amount of money spent on operations and maintenance.

Another difficult issue for superintendents is the tension that is created by the public as a result of massive budget cuts. It seems that the public wants a streamlined and lean school district but tends to react very negatively to budget cuts put in place when they are necessary to achieve such a goal. Superintendents often become lighting rods following such tumultuous decisions and can end up losing their jobs in the process (Carter & Cunningham, 1997). Issues like a slowing economy, state revenue reductions, lower property evaluations, and local demands to do more with less put superintendents in the untenable position of achieving the impossible regarding budget management. When communities realize that it cannot be done, it is often the superintendent who ends up being the "scapegoat."

One aspect of budget reduction that is usually stated initially, but does not actually play out in the long run, is the requirement to weigh the effect of any cuts on students. If the students were always considered, there might be fewer budget cuts, or none at all. In reality, almost every decision made regarding a school system should be tied to its impact on students. The expectation that superintendents can find ways to operate school systems, *and* improve them at the same time budgets are dwindling, has definitely taken a toll on the job of the superintendency. Often forced by their need to survive, superintendents may not even consider the effect budget decisions have on student learning, although educating children is usually the reason they desired the job in the first place.

A generally accepted notion is that the superintendent of schools is accountable for every facet of the school district. So in the end, it will be the superintendent who is responsible for the financial planning that keeps the district from overspending (Hayes, 2001). Thus, when a problem occurs that is manifested in a shortfall of revenue or overexpenditure of the budget, fingers tend to point directly at the superintendent, and superintendents, by virtue of their position as chief executive officer, tend to overlook this behavior and accept the good with the bad. In the area of finance and budgeting, however, most states have statutes with safeguards in place against unbalanced budgets and deficit financing. Yet even with the safeguards, some districts still manage to get into financial trouble and have to take drastic measures to balance their budgets.

Most state statutes require that school boards have fiduciary responsibility for school districts. This means that school boards must have systems in place to monitor school district finances. Given this statutory position, the school board is legally responsible for assuring that all is well financially in a school district. This is not to take the superintendent off the hook or out of the loop. On the contrary, the superintendent is accountable, given the fact that the superintendent answers directly to the school board for overseeing every function of the school district. It is generally understood that administration includes advising the school board on putting suitable structures in place to monitor all aspects of the school district, including the budget. In that regard, the superintendent is accountable for assisting the board in carrying out its fiduciary responsibility. Moreover, regardless of what is stated in the law, school board members tend to turn to the superintendent when there is a breakdown in the school district's finances and budgeting.

Most school boards that understand the direct accountability for fiscal responsibility have a committee whose job it is to monitor the budget. Such committees are usually made up of two or three school board members who review revenue and expenditure performance on a monthly or quarterly basis. The committee, in turn, regularly reports its findings to the full school board.

It is common for the superintendent to be present during these committee meetings. The superintendent's role, along with appropriate staff, is to supply the committee with information. In this regard, the superintendent serves as a staff member of the board and not as a member of the committee.

Another safeguard is the legal responsibility of the school board to see to it that the school district's finances are audited on an annual basis. The main purpose of an audit is to ensure that financial reports from school district administrators accurately show the financial condition and transactions that have taken place over a particular time period (Hoyle, et al., 1998). The review is required to be conducted by an independent auditing firm selected and employed by the board, following interviews and a recommendation by the board's committee, not the superintendent. Should the superintendent make the selection, the independence of the audit could be compromised.

The audit firm is given broad freedom to study the school district's financial records. Employees, including the superintendent, are required to cooperate with requests for information. The audit takes into account issues such as whether or not the district is using generally accepted accounting practices in its financial operations. The auditors also review the budgeting process to ascertain if expenditures are in line with yearly revenue projections. Any irregularity that may surface is brought to the attention of the school board. After completing the audit, the auditing firm prepares a comprehensive written report for the school board on the financial condition of the school district. In addition to the audit being a written report to the board, it is a public document that is available to anyone who requests a copy, and it is required that the report be given orally to the school board at a public meeting. One can only wonder how a school district could get into financial trouble with such a tight monitoring system.

Depending on the size of the district, the school superintendent may be more or less involved in the day-to-day administration of financial operations. In small districts it is very common for the superintendent to be the administrator of the budget and thus know details about the school district's finances on a daily basis. In large districts the responsibility for day-to-day finance and budgeting generally lies with a professional school business manager. If that is the case, the superintendent generally expects the business manager to keep him or her informed about the district's financial matters. Yet there is always a risk that the superintendent and school board will receive inaccurate or false financial information from the business manager, and if that should happen, they will still be blamed and accused of mismanagement. The key is for large districts to employ very skilled and honest business managers. To do otherwise could have a devastating effect on a school system. Consider the following examples, which illustrate how some districts find themselves in financial trouble.

A Pile of Overdue Bills

A small and poor district of about 500 students started a financial slide and had no room to cut expenditures, due to the fact that it was already operating at "bare bones." The superintendent was serving in roles of both the superintendent and principal. Unable to afford staff for upkeep, the district was suffering from inadequate maintenance. A lack of clerical staff prevented reports from getting out on time to the state and other agencies. The average class size was several students higher than surrounding school districts. And while the tax rate was very low and had room to grow, the public had repeatedly rejected requests for an increase.

Of course the superintendent believed he was in a no-win situation. He convinced the board that things would get better. In the meantime, he asked that the board approve all expenditures, subject to funds becoming available. This juggling act continued each month as the board approved all bills "subject to funds becoming available." Before long, the overdue bills began to mount up. It got so bad that vendors threatened legal action, and services such as power and water were in jeopardy of being discontinued. Needless to say, the district accumulated a sizeable deficit position with unpaid bills. The superintendent finally resigned from the district in frustration. When a new superintendent was hired, he faced the unpleasant task of bringing the district in line by balancing expenditures with revenue, and it was a very painful road to recovery. Up to that point, the district had held the position that certified staff was untouchable except through attrition. But that could no longer be the case with the district's critical position. First, all certified staff other than classroom teachers, such as librarians, nurses, and itinerant teachers were laid off. Then class size was increased even more when some classroom teachers had to be let go. Although the new superintendent had to take some very unpopular steps, in the long run, the district was able to get back on track and gradually restore the services that were sacrificed.

Should He Be Fired?

A school district that had just employed a new superintendent learned a few days later that the business manager had miscalculated and the district would actually be receiving 25 percent less state revenue than expected. Clearly a mistake and not malicious, the business manager readily owned up to the error and made no pretense that the previous superintendent had any knowledge of it. With the business manager's admission, even the school board did not hold the previous superintendent accountable. But when the error became known, the reaction from the district staff and the public was very negative. The budget had already been approved, and it was too late to make significant cuts to cover the ensuing shortfall.

The business manager had been with the district for 10 years and had been a very skilled and loyal employee. Despite the serious error, he was viewed as an outstanding professional by his peers. But he offered his resignation, which put the new superintendent is an awkward position. The superintendent knew that accepting the resignation would quiet the critics and allow the school district to move forward with some credibility. Moreover, the staff and public would view the new superintendent as decisive and not afraid to make tough decisions.

The superintendent, however, did not take what appeared to be the easy way out. He counseled with the business manager and decided that the mistake did not warrant dismissal. The school board was supportive of the decision but cautioned that there would be backlash from the staff and public. The superintendent believed that the firing would be a severe mistake, given the fact that the business manager's skills would be of great value in ultimately resolving the shortfall for the next year. So, working together throughout that year and the next, the superintendent and the business manager made the difficult decisions that were necessary to bring the district's budget back to a balanced position.

The Financial Coverup

Another district had been enjoying what the superintendent and board thought to be a very favorable accumulated fund reserve. With wise budgeting and conservative spending the district had developed a reputation for being fiscally responsible and careful with money. An accumulated reserve is the best position that a superintendent can be in as he prepares to retire from the post, which was the case with the superintendent in this scenario. The superintendent had always given credit to his longtime and trusted business manager for being an astute financial wizard. With open and honest communication, the two had operated as a good team for several years, and naturally the school board had been pleased. In addition, the superintendent was very popular with the community and staff, and respected for his talent in dealing with the overall responsibility of the superintendency. He was especially appreciated because the district had been in dire financial straits prior to his arrival, and he worked hard to restore its tarnished image.

Two years before the announced retirement of the superintendent, the business manager of 15 years retired and a new business manager was hired after an exhaustive search. The finance director who had served under the retiring business manager also retired the same year. Thus, two important staff positions related to business and finance were staffed with new people. With minor exceptions, the new business manager performed in a manner that was acceptable to the superintendent and the board. Although there were some questions about what appeared to be a lengthy transition, the superintendent and board remained patient. It was also common knowledge that the new business manager was having some trouble communicating with and receiving timely reports from the finance director. While the superintendent and board showed some concern, the business manager assured them that he had everything under control and could handle the minor problems with the finance director.

Three months after the new superintendent had taken over, the business manager confessed that the district had been running a serious deficit for two years. The situation had been covered up by misrepresenting facts, hoping to pull the district out of the problem before it was detected. The new business manager accepted the responsibility for knowing that the finance director had not reported accurate information to him, but he thought he could maneuver through it. However the problem grew so large that he had no choice but to reveal the scheme.

The board had many questions. Foremost, they questioned whether the retired superintendent knew about the problem. The business manager confessed that he had not confided in the superintendent. They further questioned how he could have fooled the board committee that monitored the finances and budget on a monthly basis. The business manager admitted that the figures the board committee had reviewed monthly for two years had not been accurate. The school board, as well as the retired superintendent, was embarrassed of course. The new superintendent was devastated, and she was forced to take on the unpopular task of leading the district out of a hole that she or no one else had known about except the two business officials. The business manager and the finance director both resigned. The auditing firm that should have caught the manipulation of the books was relieved of its contract. And the district began its uphill journey to fiscal health with the new superintendent and new business officials.

In these scenarios, there were ultimately clear answers as to who was responsible. But the fact remains that the superintendent was accountable, as will always be the case in the eyes of the public when serious errors occur in a school district. While the superintendent can delegate routine duties such as signing purchase requisitions and ordering supplies, the district's business function is the superintendent's responsibility. The superintendent should understand the budget, the budgeting process, and the district's financial condition, and be able to communicate that information to the staff and community (Hoyle, et al., 2005; Sharp & Walter, 2004).

School systems are similar to businesses with regard to their management responsibility (Hayes, 2001). Depending on their size, school districts are often among the largest employers in an area. But one of the biggest differences between large businesses and large school districts is indeed the budget process. Even though the overall job of the superintendent is similar to that of a chief executive officer in a for-profit company, the fact remains that superintendents derive their revenue from appropriations. Although relying on appropriations makes it much more difficult to predict or control revenue, the public expects perfection from the superintendent in operating the school district. According to 10-year surveys of school superintendents in 1992 and 2000 by the American Association of School Administrators (AASA), school finance is the number one problem superintendents and their school boards face. More than 96 percent of those responding put financial issues at the top in both of those years. Superintendents also cite fiscal problems as a leading factor in restricting their effectiveness (Glass, 2000d).

The job of the school superintendent is volatile and risky, and there are many elements that may contribute to a superintendent failing in the performance of his or her duties. A superintendent is in the unenviable position of trying to figure out on a daily basis how to most effectively help schools improve in their primary mission, while at the same time dealing with an extremely critical public that is ready to dismiss its top executive should the district experience financial setbacks. If they were handling similar responsibilities in the private sector rather than a school system, superintendents would be earning 10 times the amount they do now. Yet they are heavily criticized for receiving too high of a salary.

Superintendents often resent what they consider to be unrealistic expectations by the public and frequently compare themselves to their corporate counterparts who lack such direct public pressure. When reports of corporate mismanagement and massive accounting fraud within publicly traded companies surface, shareholders can do little more than add up their losses. With the public, a superintendent will not get off as easily. In fact, more superintendents lose their jobs due to financial mistakes than from curricular, organizational, and personnel mistakes combined (Owen & Ovando, 2000).

And there is still a further cost. Financial issues are not only taking a toll on superintendents, but possibly on the superintendency. While previous AASA 10-year studies (1982 and 1992) found that a superintendent was most likely to choose to leave the field due to personal attacks, or labor negotiations and strikes, according to the 2000 study, inadequate school district financing is now the main reason a superintendent would choose to leave the superintendency (Glass, 2000d).

8

Managing Conflicts and Crises

Many onlookers view the superintendency as an impossible job. Comments such as, "I wouldn't want your job, no matter how much it paid," or "How do you continue to do this job every day and maintain your sanity?" tend to be commonly heard from people who view the superintendency up close. No one should consider the superintendency as a career without first having a clear understanding that the position brings with it almost daily conflict and crisis. There may be some exceptions, but most superintendents will agree that dealing with conflict is endemic to the office. That is why conflict management is an essential function of successful superintendents (Owen & Ovando, 2000). And there is a growing awareness among them that handling crises properly is important to their future as leaders (Carter & Cunningham, 1997).

Conflicts generally come in three forms. There is the day-to-day conflict that surfaces without warning and consumes time that might otherwise be scheduled for another purpose. There is the continuing conflict with certain internal or external publics of the school system. And the third type of conflict, one which has earned a special place in discussions of conflicts and crises, involves the superintendent and the school board. Using examples, we will discuss all three forms and will provide suggestions on how to safely navigate through each of them.

Superintendents need to be prepared to deal with critical incidents properly. Some of them hold great potential for repercussion to the superintendent, regardless of their outcomes or solutions (Carter & Cunningham, 1997). Any one of the daily conflicts faced by a superintendent could jeopardize his or her job. Some of the hot buttons that we all know about but cannot predict are: issues of sexual misconduct; values conflicts; student discipline matters; financial mismanagement; conflicts of interest; racial or diversity insensitivity; and alcohol abuse. Whenever these issues are brought to the superintendent's attention, they must be handled in such a way that the superintendent does not become part of the issue. If personally dragged into a sensitive situation, the superintendent ultimately will be put in a defensive mode in order to salvage his or her reputation or even job, depending on the severity of the charges.

A sexual misconduct charge in any form is generally a matter that deserves the attention of the superintendent, and it is crucial that the superintendent address the matter immediately or risk being held accountable for appearing to tolerate inappropriate behavior (Carter & Cunningham, 1997). If a staff member is alleged to have made inappropriate sexual advances with a student, it is most certainly an issue for the superintendent to investigate. An accusation of sexual misconduct involving staff members would also typically warrant some intervention on the part of the superintendent. A charge against one of the superintendent's staff members involving a subordinate is yet another level of sexual misconduct that requires the superintendent's personal attention. But the most serious allegation of sexual misconduct is one made against the superintendent. It is critical to the welfare of the school district to be sensitive to the broad range of unlawful behavior classified as sexual harassment and to establish procedures to minimize the district's liability. The district should also have a formal written sexual harassment policy in place that defines sexual harassment, provides examples, and includes a process for reporting such claims (Forman, 1998).

If a teacher or other staff member is accused of sexual misconduct with a student, the superintendent cannot escape the need to deal with it directly. In the case of very large school districts, some superintendents tend to think they can delegate the matter and hold staff members accountable for resolving it. While such a strategy may work, it is not likely that it will work in every instance. The charge of sexual misconduct by an employee with a student is so volatile that the superintendent will be drawn into the fray simply through public demand. Such an egregious accusation against a staff member is going to cause the public to call the superintendent to account. Given the consequences to the district for failing to act responsibly when school employees are accused of sexual misconduct, superintendents are realizing the vital need to have clear procedures to deal with such situations (Chapman & Chapman, 1997). If the superintendent has never dealt with a sexual misconduct allegation before, or has not thought through what steps should be taken, he or she should consider the following:

- Move quickly when you learn that a serious accusation has been made against an employee. A response should be given within the same day that knowledge regarding the incident is acquired.

- The superintendent or designee should interview the adult who claims there has been misconduct. During this interview, the superintendent or designee will need to have additional officials in the room. It is a good idea for the school district attorney to be in the room as an observing official.

- In the case of a charge brought by a student, a parent or guardian should be notified the same day the report is made. However there will be cases where the parent or guardian actually reports the incident to the administration on behalf of the student. Either way, permission should be requested to allow the student to discuss the incident with the investigative team in the presence of the parent or guardian.

- Determine if a union or a professional association represents the accused employee. If so, the organization should be notified immediately about the allegations. This notification is not acquiescence of responsibility but a courtesy to the organization to inform them that one of their members is being accused. The call should not be made to seek advice since any advice received from a representative organization is likely to be biased.

- The employee needs to be called in to meet with his or her immediate supervisor and one or two other responsible school officials. Those officials could be administrators in the same building or from the central office, such as the director of human resources. The employee should also be invited to bring representation to the meeting, which may be someone from the union or association, an attorney, or both. But whether the employee chooses to come alone or with representation, the meeting should be mandatory.

- During the meeting, the employee should be confronted with the accusation. Adequate time should be provided for the employee to respond. The response could be a denial, a clarification, or an admission. It is possible that the employee may decline to comment on the advice of counsel or other representatives. After hearing the employee's side of the story, or acknowledging that the employee declined to comment, the employee should be dismissed from the meeting to await results of deliberations that should occur before the end of the day.

- The superintendent, with advice of legal counsel, must determine if there is a need for further investigation. If it is determined that the accusation appears to be without merit, the employee should suffer no further inconvenience and be returned his or her job. If further investigation is deemed warranted, the employee should be placed on administrative leave with pay, pending the conclusion of the investigation.

- Whichever course of action is chosen, the superintendent should brace for criticism. If the allegation has been made by a student, dismissing the case will anger the parents. Parents tend to support their children, no matter what has happened. To place a teacher or other staff member on leave will upset the employees. Even if the employee appears to be guilty, the union will probably complain. Be mindful that unions generally criticize administrators, and administrators should expect criticism from unions.

In any of the above situations, the superintendent risks being accused of failing to recognize the seriousness of a misconduct report, or failing to report the allegations to the school board soon enough. Treating sexual misconduct too lightly aggravates the situation and inevitably leads to undesirable consequences for everyone involved (Carter & Cunningham, 1997). Sometimes the lag between the initial knowledge of the incident and the report to the school board is due to the time it takes to complete an internal investigation. Such a delay can be interpreted by the board and/or the public as a coverup, or an attempt to hide serious allegations. On the other hand, if the superintendent suspends a popular employee who is subsequently found not to be guilty, it could spell disaster. It is one thing to take the right stance, even in the face of community and employee criticism, and quite another to judge incorrectly and lose support from all sectors (Carter & Cunningham, 1997).

The school board must be kept informed at all times while the allegations are being investigated. Given the fact that board members are prohibited by law to operate in an administrative capacity, they cannot take part in the investigation. However as individuals, their opinions on the issue at hand may differ from one board member to another. Thus, the conflict has the potential to place the superintendent at odds with certain members of the school board.

A procedure similar to the one just outlined should be followed when accusations are made by one staff member against another. The difference in a case of the staff versus staff allegation is that a third party, such as a parent, does not need to give consent for interviews. Yet the superintendent should still be prepared for strong reaction. In some cases a spouse may become emotional and threaten that the administration take drastic action or suffer the consequences.

Adult staff accusations tend to put unions in an awkward position. Sometimes the union will advise the accused to seek their own attorney to avoid the conflict of having to choose sides when both parties are members of the same organization. In cases where the union opts to take a neutral position, union representatives may still elect to attend meetings.

Should a member of the superintendent's staff be accused of sexual misconduct with an employee or student, the procedure already outlined for making the proper notifications and conducting an investigation should once again be followed. District level administrators or staff members generally have no union representing them and will likely choose to be represented by a personal attorney. If the superintendent determines it is likely that the administrator is being falsely accused, the district can pay for the defense. However, if it is determined that the case is more complicated and requires further investigation, the administrator must be placed on leave pending the outcome of a more thorough investigation. In such a case, the administrator is also usually advised to seek his or her own legal counsel. Whichever decision is made, the superintendent may lose in the eyes of some constituents. To rule that the case is without merit may be judged as the superintendent protecting one of his or her own. To suspend the administrator until further investigation, or to fire the administrator, may be judged by other administrators as the superintendent bowing to pressure rather than supporting the administration.

But the most difficult situation of all is when a superintendent finds himself or herself at the center of an accusation of sexual misconduct. Unfortunately when this occurs, the superintendent generally loses, even when innocent. The school board is placed in the awkward position of having to decide whether to support and defend their superintendent, or initiate an investigation, which often out of necessity requires that the superintendent be placed on leave pending the outcome. In addition, the school district's attorney—who ordinarily works with the superintendent on a day-to-day basis—must now align directly with the school board and advise board members on what course to take regarding the superintendent. The strain of the accusation itself is usually enough to force the superintendent out of the district. Even when innocent, a superintendent with an otherwise clean record can be blindsided by such a serious charge. Perhaps there was an innocent comment made that was misinterpreted, or a touch that was not intended as a sexual gesture. It is also possible for issues to be manufactured and built solely on half-truths and innuendoes (Carter & Cunningham, 1997). Regardless, when board members are placed in a position where they have to question the actions of their chief administrator, it is difficult for the superintendent to recover. The pressure can be so great that the easiest way out is to resign rather than submit to the personal and emotional trauma of being ostracized by the community (Carter & Cunningham, 1997). A case can, however, always be made for hanging in there, especially when the superintendent is innocent. If the relationship with the school board is solid, and they as a body believe in the superintendent, it is possible that they can survive the trauma together. Still, once that stain is on the superintendent, there will always be a lingering doubt. The question that ultimately has to be answered by the superintendent is: Can he or she can be effective in the position after such an incident?

Another potential conflict that may cause turmoil for a superintendent is repercussion from student discipline. In most school districts, no matter what size, student discipline rests with school site leaders. Whether it is an elementary or a high school, the building principal is generally the administrator responsible for fairly disciplining students. For the most part, student discipline is an everyday occurrence that happens without involvement or intervention by the superintendent. Only extreme cases that may require considering expulsion from school call for the superintendent to become involved. Otherwise, student misconduct or misbehavior is an ongoing fact of school life.

On occasion, a school principal or designee will make a misjudgment or have his or her actions questioned, which will bring the incident to the attention of the superintendent. When these situations occur, the local administrator is usually accused of unfairness based on a perceived bias. The accuser is usually a parent or other student advocate who manages to elevate the accusation of unjust punishment to the level where the superintendent must get involved. The accusation could be racism, sexism, lack of due process, or even incompetence. Whatever the circumstance, when such a critical charge is made against a staff member, it generally finds its way to the superintendent and places the issue squarely in his or her court.

The superintendent must then make a judgment, but avoid responding blindly. Moving too quickly in one direction or another could result in underestimating, misjudging, or misunderstanding the conditions surrounding the issue. Proper time should be taken to go over all the facts of the case before rendering an opinion.

The superintendent needs to be prepared to find wrongdoing on the part of the staff and deal with it accordingly. Likewise, the superintendent must be ready for the possibility of having to tell the parent(s) or advocate that the administration was justified in its punishment.

Whether the decision is pro administration or pro student, it is likely to create animosity against the superintendent on the part of the losing party. If the superintendent rules against the staff, it will be viewed as taking the politically safe route over supporting a loyal employee, and the superintendent will have the added chore of applying appropriate employee discipline. When rendering an opinion in favor of the administration, the superintendent is put in the position of bearing the burden and explaining to the parent(s) or advocate why there was no evidence of bias, which stands the possibility of evoking a strong reaction from the parent(s) or advocate. Siding with the staff could also be seen as blindly supporting the administration without regard for public opinion on discrimination in student discipline. Keep in mind that there are cases which have the potential for an entire community to erupt if it is judged that a student was mistreated. And once the issue reaches the level of the superintendent, the anger and possible protest will of course be directed at the superintendent.

Ultimately, when an issue of this magnitude hits the public, the school board will unavoidably become involved. Even when the board supports the superintendent to the best of its ability, board members often give in to community pressure and may be split on whether or not community relations can be repaired under the current superintendent following such an incident. It frequently becomes so difficult for the superintendent to work effectively and regain the confidence of the board and the external publics that it is easier for both the school board and the superintendent if the superintendent resigns.

Another issue that traps a superintendent in a no-win situation is divided community values related to certain school issues. A good example to illustrate a value-laden emotional issue is the selection of appropriate reading material for school libraries. It appears to be the norm that most educators oppose censorship in any form. Thus, support for a wide variety of optional reading material is more or less to be expected when left to the discretion of library professionals. Another assumption often made is that the superintendent, as an educator, would support the liberal view espoused by the professional librarians in the school system, as well as the state and national organizations to which they belong. However it must be understood by the superintendent, if not by anyone else, that there is more than one point of view regarding reading material selection for libraries. School board members, in this instance, do not have to follow the party line that is usually advanced by librarians and other school professionals. They, like other members of the public, are often considered conservative or liberal depending on the opinions they hold. It is a rare school board where all members see issues in the same way or are always in agreement. Board members have the option to disagree with each other, with the staff, or with the superintendent. And they certainly may align themselves with segments of the public, depending on their bent.

The superintendent does not have the option to show bias in judging reading materials. The right approach for the superintendent is to draw together a committee consisting of a cross section of the community and staff, and give them the responsibility of reading the library material that is under scrutiny. This body should deliberate and decide if the reading material should be included or excluded. Once agreement is reached, the committee should notify the superintendent, who will then pass the recommendation on to the school board without personal comment. This procedure for judging library material is sound because it seeks to involve the community and staff in the decision making process. The greatest challenge may be in how to balance the committee so that the pundits cannot claim it was not a true representation of constituents and staff. Balance can be achieved in a number of ways. However in any case, the superintendent should not be involved in the committee selection process or attend any of the committee meetings.

It is best for the superintendent to simply receive the committee's recommendation, pass the same on to the school board, and stay out of the line of fire. By following set guidelines, the role of the superintendent will be clear. Although the school board may make a political decision, the pressure to accept the recommendation from a legitimate committee constituted to provide direction will be tremendous. Without such a formal procedure, taking sides on community values will cause a great deal of difficulty and may place the superintendent's job in jeopardy, no matter how well a superintendent performs his or her duties.

Superintendents can easily find themselves in trouble when districts begin to suffer from financial problems, as was discussed in chapter 7. There are usually reasons why a school district begins to reduce expenditures, or is unable to fund programs and salaries at their regular level. The challenge for the superintendent is to make sure that issues related to funding shortages are communicated in a timely manner, and fashioned in a way that makes the news clearly understood by all sectors. To do less will place the district and superintendent in the position of appearing to hide important information from the community. And communities are not very forgiving when financial situations take a turn for the worse in an environment where they were not kept informed. While the financial shortfall explanation is usually complicated, the public will reduce their discussion to simple terms that they understand and look for easy answers. Often public opinion will be split between accepting budget reductions and revamping programs. Yet others will fight to hang on to the status quo. Eventually the blame for the budget crisis is usually assigned to the school board, or the superintendent, or both. Either way, the superintendent is likely to become the lightening rod as the school board distances itself from accountability for the problem. Without skillfully communicating at every step during a fiscal crisis, the superintendent will likely become a casualty when the community and the school board come to the conclusion that the only cure for their financial woes is a fresh start with a new leader.

Another issue that could be difficult for the staff, and especially the superintendent, is an accusation or the appearance of a conflict of interest. Some of the possibilities are obvious, and it would seem that a person would be aware of them. One example is when those in leadership positions below the superintendent—decision makers such as department heads or principals—recommend members of their immediate family, or others with whom they have close relationships, to fill vacant positions. When these decision makers fall short of thinking through the ramifications of their recommendations, the superintendent will have to step in and stop any questionable practices. Nepotism in any form is not to be tolerated; any suggestion from a department head, principal, or other decision maker that a spouse or sibling fill a vacancy should be quickly rejected (Hayes, 2001). No matter how talented that person may be, there is no legitimate reason for the superintendent to accept such a recommendation. The superintendent should not only reject the recommendation based on a conflict of interest, but also question the judgment of the subordinate administrator and consider whether or not such a person should continue in a responsible leadership position.

Equally serious is the situation of a supervisor recommending the employment of a household member who may not be a relative, as would be the case in a same gender relationship. The conflict of interest implications are identical to those of a spousal relationship, and again the superintendent must reject the recommendation. In all of these cases, the superintendent will become the unpopular arbitrator of issues that should never have surfaced in the first place. A good way for a superintendent to avoid such conflicts is to spend time with supervisors and administrators explaining what is acceptable in personnel recommendations and what is not. It is definitely better for everyone involved to prevent these incidents than to deal with them when they occur. This the same attention needs to be given to new administrators as they assume their positions.

Employment conflicts seem to get the highest visibility, but there are less visible conflicts that are also worthy of mention. For example, vendors routinely offer gifts to school administrators under the guise of thanking them for allowing the company to serve the school district. This is a common practice for vendors that sell class rings, yearbooks, and commodities. It should be a standard policy that school district administrators at any level not accept gifts, regardless of value. To accept gifts invites the potential for a conflict of interest, compromising the administrator's ability to be objective when the contract for the service or goods comes up for review or renewal. Likewise, the superintendent should not accept gifts from vendors or salespeople. As in the case of lower level administrators, the only reason gifts are offered is to attempt to influence the superintendent.

A more serious issue arises when the superintendent ends up in a conflict situation that compromises his or her own position with the school board. One example would be a superintendent who has personal financial relationships with vendors or service providers and subsequently recommends them to the board for employment. Let's say that the superintendent is paid by a law firm for certain services he provides. Then, when the school board asks the superintendent to recommend a law firm for the school district's legal services contract, the superintendent mentions the firm he is already doing business with. Could this be interpreted as a conflict of interest? Yes, or at the very least, the superintendent's actions could lead to the school board and community questioning his integrity.

While superintendent employment contracts often allow for private consulting, it is never appropriate for the superintendent to recommend that the school board employ an outside entity from which the superintendent receives payment. The vendor or service provider may be the best in the business, but the recommendation is tainted because it is based on the relationship already established with the superintendent. A superintendent who gets involved in this type of conflict often loses his or her job.

Superintendents should also avoid requesting personal favors from school district employees. Believe it or not, there are stories about school district maintenance and grounds departments being required to mow lawns at superintendents' personal residences. Even worse, some superintendents have directed maintenance employees to work on construction projects at their homes. These activities are inappropriate and possibly illegal, depending on the laws of the state. And of course such behavior on the part of a superintendent can be grounds for dismissal.

Although it is prudent for the superintendent to avoid personal business conflicts, the superintendent has the additional responsibility to advise school board members about their behavior regarding personal conflicts and the dangers of accepting gifts related to their position.

This may be problematic for the superintendent in that some board members may not see their behavior as a conflict, and therefore may resent being advised. Due to the fact that board members are elected officials with no administrative duties, it is less likely that vendors will offer them gifts. A much more likely example would be some of the service providers working directly with the board, such as attorneys, auditors, and architects attempting to woo board members through overtures such as wining and dinning. While such gestures may appear to be innocent on the surface, the primary reason for such favored treatment would be to influence school board members when service contracts come up for renewal.

So the reply to offers of dinner and other favors from vendors should always be *no*. A formal school board policy against accepting gifts from vendors or service providers will clarify the district's position for school board members and make enforcement easier for the superintendent. Conflict of interest comes in various forms. Whether it is a subordinate who is involved, the school board, or the superintendent, the responsibility is the same. The superintendent is accountable and must police the staff, advise the board, and avoid the appearance of a conflict of interest in his or her own professional as well as personal life.

In the matter of racial or diversity issues, there will always be people within the organization who are insensitive to those who are different. In some cases these individuals are simply racist, and it will show in their behavior and practice. This is not an issue in all school districts, however, since many reflect a monolithic community. But in a school system or community that is racially or ethnically diverse, discussions about race and class can be explosive (Harvey, 2005a). Some members of the public will usually question the fairness of the people who work in the system. There are times where the system, through its agents, such as teachers or administrators, will be guilty of racial or ethnic discrimination. When that happens, the superintendent needs to acknowledge that the possibility of discrimination does exist and not just blindly support the person or system that practices discriminatory behavior. It is often easier to simply back the staff and assert that none of them would ever discriminate against students or parents. While this approach will boost the superintendent's popularity with the staff, it will do little good in solving what could be a deep-seated problem of discrimination in the school district.

The most courageous position for the superintendent to take when there are charges of discrimination is to conduct a legitimate investigation and prepare for the findings to go either way, no matter who is affected. This involves anticipating the need to structure a remedy and possible discipline. Such an approach requires the superintendent to be very balanced with regard to his or her own position on racial and ethnic diversity and to model appropriate behavior. Subordinates generally take their cues from their leader, so if the superintendent of schools appears to be callous and insensitive, subordinates will assume they have permission to act similarly. Like with other sensitive issues, the school board should know where the superintendent stands on the issues of racial and ethnic diversity. And when it is observed that a school board member may be less than tolerant, the superintendent should discuss the matter privately with the board member to assist him or her in finding balance with regard to school board decisions that have the potential to affect a diverse student body.

One issue that leaves little room for negotiations is the incidence of alcohol abuse by professional educators within the school system. This does not include people who may abuse alcohol on a regular basis outside of their professional life and are never detected. There is some indication that there are a number of closet alcohol abusers who seem to continue a normal routine without detection. However in the case of teachers and other staff reporting to work in an inebriated condition, or becoming inebriated during the day, there is no room for tolerance. Abuse of alcohol and school leadership are absolutely incompatible. Some alcohol abusers recognize that they have an illness and often admit their problem before it becomes an issue, thereby neutralizing any disciplinary action. But when a supervisor detects the problem first, it generally is too late to use illness as a defense. Generally speaking, alcohol abuse at any level is grounds for dismissal in school settings, as it is not acceptable to continually employ abusers.

The consumption of alcohol by a school superintendent could pose a particular dilemma. As the district leader, the superintendent occupies a unique position. Superintendents are viewed as public figures (Blumberg & Blumberg, 1985). And like any public figure, their behavior is constantly monitored (Kowalski, 1999), they are often held to a higher standard, and they are judged on almost a daily basis. Some superintendents do not use alcohol in any form and some are moderate, social imbibers. While other staff members may self-report alcohol abuse as an illness, the same defense is not likely to help the superintendent retain his or her job. Even at informal gatherings, the superintendent is still an official representative of the school district (Kowalski, 1999). The public is generally not very understanding or forgiving when a superintendent is suspected of alcohol abuse, and as such, any accusation of alcoholism can plague a superintendent from position to position and cause otherwise viable opportunities to disappear.

The best personal rule that a superintendent can follow is to avoid drinking alcohol in public altogether. This may seem extreme and even difficult for some superintendents who contend that alcohol consumed in moderation is acceptable. But the fact is that no rumors can evolve about soberness or the lack thereof if the superintendent avoids alcohol completely in public settings. Whenever a superintendent drinks alcohol, there is a risk that observers will spread misleading rumors about the amount of alcohol consumed. There are stories about superintendents who consumed a moderate and acceptable level of alcohol only to hear rumors reported the next day stating that they were drunk. Even fabrications such as this can lead to superintendents losing their jobs. As in many cases, the school board may only be as strong as its ability to resist public pressure in an outcry against the superintendent. Given the atmosphere surrounding a resounding call for removing the superintendent due to accusations of alcohol abuse, the result may be a no-win situation. The superintendent could be forced to resign, as well as acquire a stigma that could affect employability as a superintendent in the future.

Conflicts and crises are unavoidable in the superintendency, and school superintendents can never be quite sure of where or when a critical incident will occur (Carter & Cunningham, 1997). The real question is how does the superintendent respond, or how do resulting decisions mitigate the conflict? Most conflicts require showing good judgement, taking quick control of the situation, and communicating effectively if the superintendent is to survive the incident (Carter & Cunningham, 1997). Sometimes the welfare of individuals is at stake, and at other times the entire system may be in jeopardy. Often there is a power struggle between employee group leaders, management, and the school board, and the superintendent's reputation and future employment is frequently on the line. When faced with critical crisis-laden decisions, the superintendent must weigh the chances for winning or losing, and the cost either way. Is the result worth the turmoil? Although there may be some similarities to past situations, the circumstances regarding conflicts or crises tend to be unique. Therefore, there are no set answers for most questions about how to handle them, except that all positions and the information available must be thoroughly considered before a decision is made. And even then, the superintendent must realize that any decision, no matter how well crafted, could still backfire.

The strategy of anticipating potential conflicts and knowing how to deal with them will evolve with experience and ultimately become a part of the arsenal of tools that a superintendent uses daily. At issue is the superintendent's own integrity, as well as the confidence that the school board has in its superintendent as the person who is trusted to guide the school district. The superintendent must be seen as someone who deals fairly with everyone (Carter & Cunningham, 1997). Controversies confronting school systems often result in the superintendent being caught in the middle between groups both inside and outside the district. Successful conflict resolution is greatly enhanced when the superintendent comes across as sincere and honest. Taking a strong stand based on ethical principles when necessary will also demonstrate that the superintendent is a person of character and purpose (Hoyle, et al., 2005). In addition, the school board must be informed of conflicts before they become crises. School boards, as stated in previous chapters, never like to be surprised by situations that could have been predicted, or at least discussed beforehand. In this way, the superintendent will establish a reputation for not only being insightful, but someone who can be depended upon in times of conflict.

9

The Dynamics of Leadership and Change

It is often stated in school circles that the only constant is change. History indeed supports the fact that changes are forever occurring in the school business. Writing about the dynamics of change could consume volumes and still require updating as quickly as the ink dries. However, focusing on the leadership of the superintendent in the change process will help to narrow the topic.

The effort to improve schools across the country has created an expectation that superintendents will be agents of change (Hayes, 2001), and most superintendents come to a new superintendency with plans to make improvements in the district. After all, part of the courtship on both sides assumed that the marriage would bring with it something different from what was previously experienced. Clearly the new superintendent is not expected to do business as usual or simply stay the course. Even in cases where there might have been a long-term relationship with a superintendent whom everyone admired, the anticipation of a fresh approach abounds. Typically, the new superintendent was selected because he or she had demonstrated in past professional accomplishments that something new and good would happen with the appointment.

When convincing school boards that they are the right people for the job, superintendent candidates tend to embellish their ability to make a significant difference in a school district. Usually the candidate will have studied the district and gathered information about what is really going on in the school system. The courtship talks will include superintendent candidates flattering the board regarding the district's strengths and conveying their awareness of its weaknesses, along with their ability to fix them. The astute candidate fashions his or her responses to questions during the interview around the hot buttons that need attention.

While a superintendent candidate promises to improve a school district, or bring positive change, most realize that the job is impossible as a lone ranger. Achieving goals within a system is not a simple matter. To even have a chance at success, the superintendent must rely upon teachers, principals, parents, and others in the school system. While the superintendent will often articulate the district's goals, to establish these goals and the accompanying plans to implement them, it is necessary to include constituents from the entire school district (Hayes, 2001). Therefore, it is essential for superintendents to gain their trust. Simply put, when constituents believe a proposal for improvement meets the district's needs, when they see that a strategy makes sense, and when they believe the superintendent is knowledgeable, trustworthy, and dedicated to the effort, they will support the superintendent (Johnson, 1996).

It is safe to assume that most school systems are in need of a complete review of their practices involving both internal and external publics. But depending on what type of change is needed, one sector of the district or another will be called upon for participation. It is often less difficult for the superintendent to convince the external public that change is needed than it is to influence the attitudes and practices of teachers and principals. In a system where there is a visible breakdown with regard to quality, it is the external public that generally sounds the alarm first. And by extension, the school board tends to reflect the concerns of its constituents. On the other hand, teachers and site administrators are usually vested in the current practice and are not always attuned to the need for change. Furthermore, such staff generally believes that worthwhile change emerges from classrooms and schools, and not the central office. And they tend to act on that belief, rejecting and even sabotaging what they consider to be top-down proposals that often do not reflect classroom concerns. For restructuring to be successful, everyone must be involved. A sense of organizational community can only originate when employees are informed about how they contribute to the process of school reform (Dunn, 2001). Superintendents who aspire to success must find ways to engage teachers, principals, and other staff in the discussion. To be most effective and create conditions that are essential to strategies for change, superintendents must also show genuine respect for expertise beyond the central office and treat teachers and principals as peer professionals (Kowalski, 2001).

How to go about leading in a way that is effective and successful is not a package that a superintendent can transport from one school district to another. Each school district also has a unique history which affects what a superintendent can accomplish. Besides understanding the times in which they live, new superintendents must also understand the particular history of the district (Johnson, 1996). To be sure, a superintendent needs to study and learn the lay of the land before moving too hastily and chance making costly mistakes. In any district, the superintendent is likely to encounter skepticism about his or her motives. After all, the superintendent is the new kid on the block, and for a time will be thought of as an outsider.

Most standard organization charts do not give clear direction to a superintendent about what is actually happening in a school district. Yet it is crucial for a superintendent to genuinely understand the relationships within the district for successful planning and problem solving (Hoyle, et al., 2005). It is only after the superintendent digs deep into the organization that an understanding of the true workings of the system is revealed. An effective way for a new superintendent to get a fix on how the district really operates, and to begin forming supportive relationships if they are to be successful, is to interview a large number of people very early in assuming the job (Carter & Cunningham, 1997). These interview sessions will pay the greatest dividends if the superintendent spends more time listening than talking. Although listening is a skill not usually considered crucial for job performance, it is for a superintendent, who must spend a great deal of time listening to many different interests (Hoyle, et al., 2005). Some meetings should be set up with individuals while others should be held with groups. The superintendent would be wise to meet with top-level staff individually. Staff members at the top tend not to think of themselves as belonging to a group, even though they are likely to be a part of the superintendent's inner circle. In addition, individuals at that level will have varying points of view on similar issues and the superintendent can benefit from their diverse thinking.

Interviews can also be held with employee groups. Prior to deciding on the employee groupings, the superintendent should ascertain whether the employee group leaders, such as those who head the unions, want to participate in selecting the individuals who will meet with the superintendent. It would be wise for the superintendent to comply with whatever opinion the employee group leaders have with regard to putting together groups involving their members. The leaders themselves may wish to represent their membership at the meeting rather than assigning rank and file members. The number of meetings held should reflect the number of groups identified in the school district. Meetings can take place in traditional settings, such as around a table in a conference room, or be held off site as breakfasts or luncheons if that is more convenient for the participants.

Again, these meetings should be billed as sessions where the new superintendent gets to know the people within the district. During these meetings patterns will begin to emerge. These patterns that will tell the story of what the real issues are in the district, in the opinion and experience of the various employees and employee groups. As stated earlier, the district's formal structure may be quite different from its functioning structure. One challenge the superintendent will have—among many others—after these sessions have concluded is deciding whether the formal system is worth salvaging or whether it should be restructured. If the current organization is found to be functioning poorly, it needs to be communicated to all concerned that change will occur, but not just for the sake of change.

Further, it should be highlighted that the series of listening sessions held with the various individual and groups of employees will serve as the catalyst for reexamining how the administrative delivery system functions. The informal survey of employee opinions is a powerful step and must be acknowledged as a building block that is absolutely necessary. Additional and specific input may be solicited prior to drawing up and announcing a new organizational plan. Once a new system has been decided upon, the challenge will be for that system to actually serve the employees. A new superintendent will score a lot of points if the employees perceive the change as a response to their observations and concerns. It is also viewed positively when a new superintendent loses no time in providing remedies that work. In the grand scheme of working through a change process, sufficient time must be taken to implement the new system properly and the various steps need be methodically measured. Yet there are some issues, such as violations of the law, that require taking swift action. The chances for success will typically depend on the superintendent's ability to quickly diagnose a situation and make assumptions that lead to corrective action.

In today's educational leadership environment, the various publics tend to interpret "change" as the opportunity for the district to involve them. This attitude is supported when a superintendent at least has a mindset that includes having various stakeholders play a meaningful role. And it is exhibited when the superintendent sets out early to understand the unique features of the community and gather some ideas on which approaches are most likely to result in effective change. A change process in contemporary parlance features a superintendent who values involvement by all parties that are significant to the educational enterprise. Yet this involvement is not as simple as what was considered acceptable in the past. At that time, a superintendent sought input before making important decisions but often controlled the input based on whose opinions were sought. In such a model, some constituent groups were left out of the loop, or through lack of involvement were deemed unimportant.

Superintendents today should have a doctrine of leadership that is clearly stated and understood by the internal and external publics. Too often leadership philosophy can be confused with what some people refer to as *vision* or *mission*. Once again, vision can be defined as the mental image of an organization's past and it's ideal future (Kowalski, 1999), while mission describes the work that needs to be done to make the vision happen (Townsend, et al., 2005). These terms, depending on the school district, are sometimes used interchangeably. In other places the terms are used exclusively. Neither should be used in a context that indicates the superintendent is expected to singularly bring a vision or mission to a school system. At best, the superintendent will come to the job with deep philosophical ideas about leadership, among which is the need for the district to have a clear vision and mission.

While the district must provide an overall vision for the schools and clearly articulate that vision among the many interests within the district, this is a shared vision that addresses the needs of students and the community while upholding high standards. So instead of arriving with his or her own game plan, the superintendent must help those with a legitimate role to play collaborate together to develop a vision for change in response to local needs, by promoting the open exchange of ideas and encouraging others to act cooperatively. Success will depend on individual groups understanding one another's positions and agreeing on a shared vision (Carter & Cunningham, 1997).

A good beginning philosophy for a superintendent is to have the school community totally involved and a process in place to prove it. There are several approaches that could be taken, all of which require a great deal of time and skill on the part of the leader. Among the suggestions is a complete reassessment of the internal communications processes. Part of this assessment involves determining whether anyone within the organization has been left out of the current communications loop that ultimately benefits the superintendent by providing input on the thoughts of employees pertaining to certain matters. Setting up a structure for all groups to have direct and regular contact with the superintendent, regardless of the size of the district, can pay off well in the long run. For such an open process to be successful, the superintendent cannot be intimidated by the prospects of those in lower level positions being able to communicate directly to the top eschelon. Sometimes when this approach to openness with lower level employees or administrators is taken, administrators at the level closest to the superintendent feel threatened. But after all, even in traditional leadership styles, some administrators have the ear of the superintendent and others in the organization do not.

Public schools have historically followed a management model with centralized or concentrated power at the top (Hoyle, et al., 2005). However top-down leadership does not inspire creativity or cooperation in others, which is what must take place if change is to happen within a school system (Johnson, 1996). The superintendent must determine, with the constituents, that shared decision making is instead valued. Like any important change, the chances for success in moving from a top-down military model to a model of shared decision making requires a common understanding of what it means. What it does mean is just as important as what it does not. It does not mean that the superintendent and school board are abdicating responsibility for their respective roles. This actually cannot occur since most laws are clear with regard to the legal responsibility of the superintendent and the school board. What it does mean is that the superintendent and school board value the opinions of the various components of the system and are creating a formal process whereby meaningful input from everyone is not only allowed but encouraged on important decisions affecting the school district. Moreover, to be successful, it needs to be demonstrated that the system works, through evidence and not just rhetoric.

One way the shared decision making model is made visible is through what has been loosely referred to in many places as *site-based decision making* or *site-based management*. Site-based management is a strategy used to improve education by transferring sufficient authority and the responsibility for making decisions to individual school sites (Norton, et al., 1996). While it can vary in form from school to school (Sharp & Sharp, 2004), many forms of site-based management have been implemented in thousands of school districts (Glass, 2000d). As stated earlier, this is not to imply that the responsibility for making decisions is given away. It does, however, require a formal system so that meaningful participation will lead to quality decisions that will be supported by everyone involved. Furthermore, site-based management assumes that primary involvement, autonomy, and control of resources by those closest to the children contributes to better decisions and consequently improved student results (Weiss, 1993). This approach can include assigning to sites absolute power over how a particular block of money is spent, or what process is used to select instructional materials. But whichever approach is used, the parties involved, including the school board, all need to understand and agree on the parameters.

Shared decision making, or site-based management, can demonstrate what has come to be known as *collaborative leadership,* which emphasizes the importance of individual values and actions. Collaboration is more than cooperation (Harvey, 2005b). Collaboration provides the superintendent with a chance to seek out and accommodate opposing viewpoints early in the process and later avoid resistance at critical junctures (Johnson, 1996). Collaborative leadership by a superintendent is often tested when employee unions try to challenge the sincerity of the approach. As mentioned earlier, some sectors of the school system will interpret or even desire that collaborative or shared leadership to be a mechanism for exchanging power from the leader to the followers. Care must be taken by the superintendent in situations where employee unions may push to share in decisions that could potentially harm the school district. For example, if the teachers' union was allowed to control class size, that would make it impossible for the superintendent and the school board to cut expenditures in times of reduced school funding. To avoid having disputes about which decisions can be shared and which cannot, guidelines need to be set before the superintendent or school board embarks down the shared decision making path.

The spirit of openness, by whatever name, can be extended to other sectors of the school community with success as well. One way to involve the entire community is to develop a strategic planning process. There are many approaches to strategic planning and the key is to find the method that will work best for a particular school district. Strategic planning, simply stated, is setting meaningful goals for an organization in a systematic way so that the process of development, implementation, and monitoring will produce the desired results for improvement. The goals should serve two purposes: to provide direction and to create a sense of ownership by the constituents in both the process and the end product (Owen & Ovando, 2000). Obviously there are other definitions for strategic planning, depending on what the goal is for the organization. But this definition seems to fit well for school districts seeking a wide range of improvement.

Although the superintendent is the key person in the strategic planning process, successful strategic planning requires including all district constituents (Norton, et al., 1996). Every stakeholder in the district should either directly or indirectly have an opportunity to provide input (Hoyle, et al., 2005). At its inception, a strategic planning process should invite all constituent groups to be involved. The invitation from the school board and superintendent should include reasons why a strategic plan is important and why there is a need for widespread participation. A good strategic planning process is made better by securing a third party, preferably a professional facilitator, to conduct planning sessions with the participants. There is no standard length of time required to take the strategic plan from start to finish. Planning varies with the model used; a plan can be developed over the course of a few days to several months. Often the time required to complete a strategic plan depends on the number of participants and the time available for meetings. The bottom line is that the plan is complete when directions are produced that represent the desires of the participants.

Many school districts and superintendents have undertaken strategic planning. However it is not uncommon to hear about school districts that complete the process but never make it to the progress phase. The progress phase, for this purpose, is the implementation plan. A good implementation plan will feature time lines and benchmarks for accomplishing the various recommendations that flow from the planning process. The school board and superintendent should assure the volunteers that their effort is serious and that they are not wasting their time. The operative posture that should come from the school board is that there is commitment from the top to follow through. This commitment must be stated up front and backed by an action of the board to allocate the resources required to implement the plan once it is developed.

The implementation plan should be very specific and provide details about annual progress evaluations. Furthermore, once a strategic plan is adopted, the district is actually saying to the staff and public, "This is how we are going to do business for the next five years." To adopt such a position will leave little room for doubt about whether or not the plan will be funded. In the most basic interpretation, from adoption of the plan to the end of the five years, all activities that happen within the school district should reflect the plan. If this is not the case, then the plan is not a true strategic plan. A true strategic plan guides all the activities of the school district until the plan's implementation is completed. After completion, which is typically five years, the plan is updated to reflect another time period for implementation, which is usually another five years.

If the plan is comprehensive, it will serve as the implementation tool for all important facets of the school system. A typical plan will address areas such as:

- Accountability

- Administrative organizational structure
- Budget planning
- Class size
- Communications
- Community involvement
- Curriculum development
- Diversity plans for student assignment and staffing
- External relations
- Facilities utilization
- Goals for student achievement
- Internal relations
- Staff development
- Student discipline
- Textbook adoption

While this list is not all-inclusive, it gives a flavor for how such a plan connects all aspects of a school system. As part of the strategic plan, a list of statements are developed that define the improvements that are needed and detail what is expected in each of the categories above. The statements are then committed to a matrix that covers a multiyear implementation plan, and the plan becomes the catalyst for rebuilding the school district to reflect the desires of the school community.

It takes skill and determination for a superintendent to embark on strategic planning as the tool for doing business in the school system. The skill comes in convincing all parties of the importance and value of the tool. The determination comes in the superintendent's ability to keep the district on course once the plan is adopted so that it indeed becomes the planning tool for all activities and actions within the system. Frequently the plan falls by the wayside if the leader is not strong enough to make sure that it does not end up on the shelf as just another fad that came and went. An obvious goal in any good strategic plan will be community involvement in the school district. With public concerns for education at supposed record levels, and the public giving education the highest priority, school district administrators have to show respect to diverse groups and their demands for greater representation and participation in the decision making process (Institute for Educational Leadership, 2001). In order for a good school system to meet the educational goals of a community, the superintendent needs to get to know the community and understand its unique characteristics. Too often school districts have taken the easy route and developed traditional structures involving the community, such as districtwide citizens advisory committees and parent and teacher associations at the building levels. These structures are excellent tools for involvement, however by themselves they are woefully inadequate. Still, some superintendents consider this the safe approach to community and school involvement.

In today's environment we acknowledge that traditional leadership structures do not begin to address or establish linkages with the entire community, and to bypass sectors of the community is no longer acceptable for a progressive school system. Either we are serious about implementing effective community relations programs or we are not. If we are serious, we will survey the organized groups within the school district and ascertain which community leaders may be connected to those groups. The local chambers of commerce would be a good place to start to develop such a roster. As stated in an earlier chapter, a number of special interest groups will be identified, from which a cadre of community advocates will emerge. Such involvement will punctuate the sincerity of the district's leadership in seeking meaningful community involvement.

School systems all across the country are recognizing that in order to be responsive to an increasingly demanding public, fundamental change in how they do business must take place. The first step in achieving the necessary change in a system is for the school board to desire change, which is generally a manifestation of its responsiveness to its constituents. Of course to assemble a school board that is monolithic in its thinking is unrealistic. It is realistic, however, that a school board can agree on the one mission that should have brought board members to their office—to provide the best education possible for the students they serve, given the available resources. There are several ways a school board can demonstrate the seriousness of this quest. The board can pass a policy that requires all actions taken by the board reflect the advancement of student achievement in a positive way. Or, as we have discussed, the district can implement a strategic plan to guide all the actions that occur within the school system. Both of these approaches seem simple enough, given a school board that is committed to working on behalf of the public to maintain the highest standards possible in the school system. Yet with the competing interests that school board members face in their personal lives and the limitations imposed by law, they cannot always insure that their mission will be carried forth.

The best way for a school district to experience meaningful change and stability in relation to needed reform is to employ an accomplished and courageous superintendent of schools. For a district to be successful in the change process, the superintendent must be passionate and persuasive in promoting innovation and change. Good superintendents recognize that the power of a clear vision of excellence can be more effective than the power granted through the authority of an office. It is extremely helpful if the superintendent is well-grounded in the teaching and learning process so that credibility with classroom teachers is not in question.
In some districts across the county, non-traditional superintendents have been employed as an experiment. But those have tended to be desperate attempts to find some new approach to revive troubled school systems.

School boards in search of a superintendent need to stay focused and remember that it is classroom teachers who inevitably will make the difference in whether or not students learn. To that end, securing a talented superintendent who is first an educator seems to make good sense. Superintendents and their staff, working with teachers, will assist school district leaders in understanding the latest thinking about effective teaching practice. Such collaboration on the improvement of instruction will ultimately play a large role in the process of reforming schools. Moreover, a good superintendent will be a voice for the people, while the school board is generally the voice of the people. As a voice for the people, the superintendent is heard in many ways: through community involvement; speaking at civic functions; in articles and columns in newspapers; on radio programs with call-in features; on commercial and cable television; by visiting classrooms; and through other appearances that place the superintendent in front of large numbers of people.

In providing direction for the change needed in a school system, a superintendent should be well-versed in the many issues that are connected to school improvement. In addition, the best superintendents are able to demonstrate that school system reform can be a reality. A good superintendent leads by modeling the professional discourse that should be a mainstay in a school district (Hayes, 2001). Modeling truthfulness, honesty, and openness with employees is more likely to lead to an informed and supportive district staff. Superintendents who display these characteristics are also more inclined to earn the support of a community trying to form an opinion about the person they are entrusting with the education of their children (Hoyle, et al., 2005). Surrounded by the desires that countless others have for their leadership, superintendents are expected to formulate education visions that inspire and guide constituents to improve their schools. However they need to realize both the limits and the potential of the superintendency, strategically balancing their authority with their reliance on others, and work to build broad support for shared leadership and collaborative change (Johnson, 1996).

10

Political Savvy and the Superintendency

The position of superintendent of schools, with a few exceptions across the country, is a nonelected public office (Glass, 2000d). City or town managers, park district directors, library directors, and police chiefs are other examples of appointed public officials. What's common among these positions is that they are administrative in nature, and they are appointed by boards, councils, or commissions. The parallel of these jobs to the superintendency, depending on the size and complexity of the municipality, tends to be with their appointment through a body of elected officials. Elected positions are inherently political and are attained through a political process. Once these individuals are elected to boards, councils, and commissions, they serve at the pleasure of the general population that elected them, or the constituent base that they appealed to in order to get elected. Therefore, they are beholden to the electorate and must act according to the expectations of their support base or risk not being reelected.

Before exploring the contrast of the superintendency to elected officials, it would help to define *politics* for this discussion. A simple definition generally given for politics is "the art of compromise," or what is generally known as the ability of the person holding the political position to give and take. A good politician knows that you cannot win all of the time. There needs to be a balance in knowing when to hang on and when to let go. Some politicians are skilled at seeking the middle ground and looking for the win-win. Understanding the workings of politics depends on your view of the political system and the various political personalities. Some people see politics as negative, no matter who the players are, and it is not uncommon to hear politics described as crooked or dirty. Others accept politics as a fact of American life and choose to work within the political process to achieve their goals or advance their agenda. However viewed by the public, it is clear that elected officials have no recourse but to perform in a political arena and need to keep a sharp ear to the ground so they will know when they are representing the interests of the people who elected them to the office and when they are not.

In contrast, the superintendent of schools is appointed in most parts of the country, as stated earlier. Unlike other nonelected management positions, except for managers of large cities, the office of the superintendent of schools is by design a *chief executive officer* position. More often than not, the superintendency is the most highly visible position in town, and when compared with both private and public organizations, the school district is actually the largest employer (Harvey & Wallace, 2005) with the largest budget (Carter & Cunningham, 1997). It is also not uncommon for the superintendent to be the highest paid public official in the area. Because members of the general public do not always understand the difference in roles, the superintendent is sometimes viewed as a member of the school board. As a result, some citizens really do not comprehend how the superintendency relates to politics.

After all, the public sees the superintendent sitting with other people at a table where important decisions are made. To the uninformed observer, all of the people serve the same function. Although the board president tends to be the person chairing the meetings, at some point the superintendent will usually make a report or voice an opinion on any number of issues. So to many laypeople, the superintendent may appear to be a powerful political figure. The fact remains however, that the superintendent is an employee, hired by an elected school board. By definition, as a nonelected official, the superintendent is not a politician.

If you were to ask superintendents how they see their role in the political process, the answer will likely depend on which superintendent is answering the question. But most superintendents would say that they are not politicians and would prefer not to be viewed as such. As a matter of fact, when veteran superintendents give advice to aspiring or novice superintendents, they usually warn the aspirant to be careful with politics. This is usually stated in the context that a superintendent should not appear to be a politician or political player in the eyes of the staff or the public. They would probably add that a superintendent who gets involved in the politics of the school board and/or the school system is likely to get in trouble and risk losing their job. On the other hand, most experienced and successful superintendents will tell you that a good superintendent is well aware of the ongoing political issues within a school system.

While throughout their careers superintendents have been advised to not take part in political activities, they have little choice but to be involved. They continue to be forced to interact with elected officials, special interest groups, and board members who expect them to respond to multiple and diverse demands, which requires political insight and expertise to make wise decisions (Blumberg & Blumberg, 1985). The skill, they will say, lies in the superintendent's ability to work the political process without getting into the fray. This balance is so difficult, and different from school system to school system, that it is nearly impossible to give advice on how it can consistently be achieved.

The reality is that school superintendents from time to time do engage in the political processes that are necessary for the function of their organizations. School districts are not self-sufficient. Their concerns are entangled with the interests of government, business, community groups, and social agencies. Political involvement is so fundamental to the work of today's superintendents that they cannot succeed as educational leaders without taking an active role in district politics (Johnson, 1996). But the political processes in which an astute school superintendent engages are quite different from the politics of elected officials.

The school superintendent does not get involved in politics to please a political constituency and get reelected, but rather to build coalitions to advance the school system. In order to accomplish this, the superintendent needs to lead those who have a stake in the school system to recognize their shared interest in the system's success (Owen & Ovando, 2000). It's not about the superintendent, it's about the school district.

Selected for their expertise and experience in school leadership, superintendents can be more effective if they are able to develop a supportive constituency among the school board, internal organizations, professional staff, and the community, which includes the political power structures. Building this coalition and maintaining a stable base of support for the educational initiatives of the school district is in fact the political work of the superintendent, who takes on the role of statesperson (Carter & Cunningham, 1997). Effective school leaders use politics as another tool to achieve goals through their relationships with other people (Ramsey, 1999).

The best school superintendents, as previously stated, are good educators first. A solid background as a successful educator is extremely helpful when it comes to having the credibility needed to demonstrate to the professional staff that there is a clear understanding and appreciation for teaching (Kowalski, 1999), and that learning is the district's main focus. And while the required skills that separate the superintendent—conceptually and functionally—from other educators form a very long list, all the educational expertise and knowledge of problems surrounding teaching and learning may be for naught if the superintendent does not have the political know-how to manage his or her own position in today's difficult and conflictive climate (Carter & Cunningham, 1997). In this regard, the superintendent is quite alone, and in an uncomfortable spot at that. On one hand he or she must work with the school board as its expert, and on the other hand the superintendent must maintain the support of the staff as one who fully understands and cares about what happens in the classroom (Hayes, 2001). Then there is the community, with its various faces. The business community is typically interested in whether or not the superintendent is astute enough to create a working relationship with them. And the general public has similar expectations. To be sure, school district politics can be especially complex because of so many diverse political agendas competing for recognition (Ramsey, 1999).

The news media usually want personal attention from the superintendent as well. As a rule, media sources tend to assign beat reporters to cover the day-to-day school district matters, with occasional special assignments to investigate specific issues within the school district. Regardless of whether the story is routine or a special assignment, most of the time reporters request a response from the superintendent. No matter how large or small the school district, the superintendent is the district's chief spokesperson (Hayes, 2001; Hoyle, et al., 2005). It is important for the superintendent to speak with reporters and return phone calls. As a rule of thumb, it is better to be part of a story than to read information in the paper the next day that could have been clarified, or hear that "the superintendent was unavailable for comment" or "had no comment." To read or hear those words used often gives the impression that the district is holding back information (Hayes, 2001). It is better for the superintendent to explain why he or she cannot answer a reporter's question than to avoid them (Kowalski, 1999). Beyond the beat reporters, it is expected that the superintendent will develop relationships with media outlet executives. Without such relationships, the district runs the risk of the media becoming adversaries. Part of the political responsibility of the superintendent is to work with the media so that they are allies. Simply put, fair media coverage should be the superintendent's goal (Hayes, 2001). A wise superintendent will need no prompting to treat the media as partners and trust them with advance information about the school system.

The subject of political savvy for the superintendent would be remiss without giving some attention to the responsibility of the school superintendent to be in tune with elected officials at the state level. Typically these officials are state representatives and senators. A superintendent who is not aware that legislators spend a great deal of their time discussing education is a superintendent who lives in a vacuum. Debate about schools at the state level tend to be quantitative—it all comes down to numbers. The questions asked of and by legislators usually concern test scores and how much of the state's money is being spent or requested by public schools. The general public wants to hold the legislature accountable for how money is spent on various state agencies, and the public school system, in this context, is an agency of the state. State legislators therefore need to know details regarding what is occurring in school systems across the state, which puts the school superintendent in the best position to develop and maintain the necessary relationships to keep legislators informed, and to give advice when warranted. The savvy superintendent will become personally acquainted with the legislators who represent the territory covered by the school district and create political ties that can pay off big for the school system.

In a word, superintendents survive or fail based on their ability to manage the politics of the school system's many facets. Political acumen on the part of the superintendent is so embedded in the role that the superintendent needs to give considerable thought and decide how each encounter should be addressed. A primary responsibility of the superintendent is handling competing expectations, numerous political agendas, and diverse ideas without unnecessarily creating enemies or distrust (Carter & Cunningham, 1997). At times, superintendents find themselves in no-win situations in which any significant decision they make will alienate or upset someone or some group. Successful district and community politics is based on finding a compromise between what the district and the community desires. If that point can be found and accepted by both parties, the superintendent is more likely to be viewed as effective by the board and the community (Hoyle, et al., 2005). Unlike elected politicians, superintendents do not have partisan coalitions they can rely on when in trouble. Elected politicians have the safety of their office until the next election, while the superintendent must always be conscious of how his or her actions are viewed by the school board. Given the potential gravity of an unpopular decision, the superintendent remains vulnerable and constantly faces the possibility of being removed from office by the school board.

To be effective, today's superintendent must be an adept student of politics, and for a superintendent, school system politics tend to go beyond the basic definition stated earlier. The politics practiced by astute superintendents are the politics of strategic involvement. Carefully negotiating these politics will place the superintendent in the best position long term. The politics the superintendent needs to avoid are partisan politics, or seeking political alliances with key players. The superintendent should refrain from aligning with a political party or a political faction of the school board. Political parties tend to move in and out of power, and school board factions will ultimately change, which can leave the superintendent's job in jeopardy if the superintendent takes sides. Playing partisan politics and/or siding with a school board faction are simply serious mistakes.

Although though the political skill of working through the maze of power and influence may be a part of negotiating with all constituent groups, two major political challenges for the superintendent remain: the school board and the unions. Conflicts between superintendents and school boards can surface at any time. Therefore, the superintendent must establish the boundaries of a working relationship with board and others in the system. The skilled superintendent will permit school board members to perform their duties as policy makers and representatives of their constituency without allowing them to encroach on classroom or administrative issues. But in practice, board members sometimes stray from policy to administrative functions, either as a group or individually (Norton, et al., 1996). The worst reputation that a school board can have is one of micromanagement. Micromanagement is often the result when board members are unclear as to their roles and responsibilities (Institute for Educational Leadership, 2001). An effective superintendent will spend quality time, at retreats and other forums, counseling school board members on their role so that there will be no misunderstanding with regard to their function.

Yet the members on some school boards more than others find it difficult to understand and/or agree on their designated role. In those instances an astute superintendent will recognize the need to compromise with the board on points where it is allowed within state law. What the superintendent should guard against, if possible, is a clash between what the board believes is its role versus its legal role. But it is up to the superintendent to determine in early discussions whether or not he or she can create a cooperative relationship with the board. If the situation becomes impossible, only the superintendent is to blame. Candidates should not accept the position of superintendent unless they conclude that they can work with the board offering the job.

School boards, of course, do change. In the case of a change that is significant enough to completely alter the relationship between the board and the superintendent, the superintendent often chooses to leave the district before being forced out. A new school board majority may not give the superintendent the option to change direction and/or conform to its agenda. They tend to ask the superintendent to leave, or in worst case scenarios, they may take a public action to fire the superintendent. At best, a superintendent and board will reach an understanding of their roles and avoid conflict. Too often, however, the initiative to keep the balance falls to the superintendent. And despite everyone's effort at maintaining harmony, there will be issues on which the superintendent and the board disagree. The key for the superintendent is to avoid destructive public conflict and strive to frame responses in a way that will not embarrass board members. If a board member misspeaks and is not corrected by the board president, it is often better for the superintendent to let the comment pass until the matter can be discussed with the board president and the board member. Handled properly by the superintendent, the issue can be corrected at the next meeting without pointing out the board member's error in public.

Besides the school board, the other major political challenge for school superintendents is working with employee unions (Hayes, 2001). In most public education systems it is the teachers' union that is the most difficult. The relationship between the superintendent and the union will undoubtedly be influenced by the school district's labor relations history (Johnson, 1996). And like the school board, the superintendent needs to make the effort at the beginning of his or her tenure to get to know union leadership. Unions, especially teachers' unions, can be very demanding of the superintendent's attention. Even when union leaders may dislike the superintendent personally, they still expect the consideration they believe is due their organization.

Unions, by design and perhaps by training, are institutions that seem to thrive on conflict. The view in some circles is that without conflict, the union is not relevant. True or not, a good superintendent cannot afford to structure a relationship in which the union is the enemy. Superintendents hoping to improve the education in their districts need the support of teachers, which is almost impossible to obtain if labor-management relations are hostile, or if union leaders discredit the superintendent (Johnson 1996). Therefore it is essential that superintendents establish fair and respectful relationships with union leaders. To create a positive relationship takes political knowledge and will always be viewed as delicate by the unions. Union leaders, after all, are elected officials and often relate more to elected school board members than the superintendent. When a superintendent is successful in establishing good relations with union leadership, it is still expected that the union will continue to see its role as relating to the school board. The school board, however, generally expects the superintendent to act as its representative and maintain good relations with the unions (Norton, et al., 1996). Like some of the other groups, the teachers' unions tend to work the school board politically. So the superintendent should not be surprised when union leaders try to speak with the board directly on some issues, even though they know the superintendent has the answers. They seek a connection with the school board because board members are elected officials, and a political link can only aid their cause. Also, it tends to build stature with union members when union leaders can get the ear of the board.

A superintendent who relates well with the unions tends to take the pressure off the school board to deal with them directly. Moreover, school boards are aware of the political nature of teachers' unions, and the fact that they are capable of attempting to divide the board by seeking audiences with individual board members. Given the behavior of unions, the superintendent is often caught in the middle between them and the school board (Hoyle, et al., 2005). Union relationships can be volatile, with a struggle for power and authority over who is going to make the educational decisions. This reality is borne out by the history of collective bargaining in schools. Negotiated contracts have steadily expanded beyond salary, benefits, and basic working conditions, and have encroached on issues relating to class size, curriculum, and organizational structure. The struggle for power by definition makes the relationship adversarial. But the superintendent, as stated earlier, cannot afford to treat union leaders with disrespect. In the politics of the school system, the superintendent will sooner or later need the support of the employee unions. Board members, on the other hand, watch and expect that the superintendent will maintain relationships that promote harmony in the school system.

A savvy superintendent will recognize that decisions need to be guided by sound educational principles and purposes, but with the understanding that the teachers' union in particular will want to be a part of or influence all educational decisions. To achieve balance, the superintendent needs to establish a forum to meet with union leadership on a regular basis. Such meetings should allow open expression as much as possible so that educational issues can be discussed by both sides without reservation. It is not necessarily important that the meetings have formal agendas, but that the parties feel comfortable in bringing up any topic. It is likely that the informal, evolving discussions will reflect what is occurring in the school system.

The fact that the meetings are held often and consistently will allow the superintendent and the unions to stay current with events. While this is a structured relationship, the bonus could be that the union leaders will get to know the superintendent as a person. But even if a close and trusting relationship develops, the union will not relinquish its role as a power broker. Members will, however, respect the superintendent who respects them by taking the time to meet with union leaders and be open enough to discuss all educational issues. What needs to be avoided is allowing the meetings to resemble negotiating sessions. It is generally a skilled superintendent who keeps discussions from appearing like collective bargaining. And once the parameters have been established, union leaders are less likely to cross the line.

The centrality of politics is endemic to the position of school superintendent. Some superintendents may express frustration with the political nature of the job and the expectations that they become politically active. But the superintendents who survive ultimately grow into their political role. To be effective, a superintendent must respond to the unique political climate of the school system and establish viable relationships with all political figures, but especially the school board and the unions. Allowing all interest groups to have a voice in what takes place within the district often helps avoid conflict later, however it requires the skills of negotiation and compromise, and must be done while maintaining the trust of everyone involved. (Hayes, 2001). No longer able to choose whether or not to be involved in the political arena, superintendents must assess the politics of their districts and determine how to best work within it (Johnson, 1996).

PART III
Meet Eight Superintendents

The next eight chapters will introduce you to a variety of superintendents and the school systems to which they were appointed. Given the fact that there are nearly 16,000 school districts in the United States, it is obviously not possible to include every type. However, based on what we know about school districts, the eight superintendents highlighted here, and their districts, provide a good representation of those operating in this modern era. They will serve as a sample of the kinds and sizes of districts found across the country, and the different styles of leadership superintendents possess.

We will examine the processes and practices of these superintendents from their selection through assuming the superintendency. Comparison and contrast are used to emphasize specific expectations of these superintendents, focus on which strategies work and which may not, and see the uniqueness of the districts and school boards. Although formal leadership theory is not the focus for comparing these superintendents, the common leadership activities that led to their success or failure will be discussed.

The performance of the incumbent superintendents, as well as the behavior of the school boards prior to and following their selection of a new superintendent, are also included to better illustrate real life scenarios. A superintendent's decision to leave a district, or a board's desire to replace its superintendent often does not happen in isolation unless the superintendent is simply retiring. And even then, the superintendent may be worn out from years of successful, but stressful, service.

11

Arcadia: Opening Communication Channels

School district: Arcadia—two high schools in two different municipalities, although only about three miles apart in the first suburban ring of a large metropolitan city

Socioeconomics: Urban/suburban, mostly first-generation middle-class

Demographics: A very diverse mix of 8,000 students; 40 percent minority

Superintendent: Dr. Benjamin Abbey—comes to Arcadia with experience as a superintendent in another state

Arcadia is a community about five miles from a major midwestern city and is classified as suburban, although in appearance it resembles many of the neighborhoods that are actually located within the corporate limits of the city. The Arcadia school district is spread across parts of six independent villages, each with its own governance structure, tax rates, and assessment levels. The neighborhoods have neat, city-type homes on small lots and many apartment complexes. For the most part, Arcadia is considered a bedroom community whose residents hold professional jobs. The district is located close to important higher education institutions and major health care facilities. Most residents of the Arcadia school district work outside the corporate limits, commuting the short distance to their workplace in the major city.

Some might refer to the area as "changing," which is a euphemism for ethnic minorities replacing white residents in the neighborhoods. Like many communities in transition, the dominant white power structure remains in place, and the emerging minority population has been received with resistance—ranging from tolerance to resentment, depending upon whom you talk to. Unlike some first-ring suburban communities that are more progressive, the towns surrounding the Arcadia school district, and the schools, appear not to have a plan in place for integrating the influx of newcomers. The district does, however, have well-maintained facilities and modern equipment, the products of consistent community support for keeping the schools up-to-date. Two very large, comprehensive high schools comprise this two-building district, which is typical of many of the suburban school districts surrounding the city. Both buildings house grades 9 through 12. By tradition, the Arcadia central office has remained located in the older and more historic building. It was the only building in the district until rapid growth required construction of a second building.

The Arcadia district is clearly changing in racial demographics, with about 40 percent of the students classified as minority. Minority in this context means African American, with a small number of Hispanic students making up barely 1 percent of the school district's total population. Although many ethnic backgrounds are represented in the school district, they are ethnic only in their origin. For all intents and purposes, students with ethnic backgrounds other than African American and Hispanic are considered white. About 30 percent of the students qualify for federal lunch support, and district finances seem stable.

The school district is governed by a seven-person school board which consists of all white males. The members serve staggered four-year terms, with elections being held every other year in the spring. For many years, the local community has lived with the understanding that sitting school board members are in control of who is allowed to join the board. While elections have been open to any qualified contenders, it is general knowledge that incumbent board members seek out individuals similar to themselves and solicit their candidacy. This practice of "anointing" was very common years ago in many school districts across the country but has, for the most part, dissipated. In Arcadia, however, the system still seems to flourish. And up to this point, there has been no indication that board insiders have ever "sponsored" a woman or ethnic minority either.

Just as troubling is the board's propensity to meddle in administrative affairs. It is assumed by many district observers that the school board is the body responsible for hiring within the district. Therefore many potential employees court board members for reassurance that they will get a job without going through the application process. This micromanaging caused problems for the previous superintendent, who often challenged board members when they would turn down a recommendation he made for one of their own. Also, when the public accused the former superintendent of making bad decisions, board members often criticized him openly. The superintendent would remind the board in closed sessions that while he was not above corrections, those discussions should take place in private meetings between him and the board. His requests were to no avail; the board's negative behavior and public criticism persisted.

The Arcadia district had been growing rapidly, with enrollment reaching 8,000 students when Dr. Benjamin Abbey became the superintendent. Abbey, a 49-year-old white male, has a doctorate in educational administration from a major eastern university. Before coming to the district, he was the superintendent of schools in a kindergarten through grade 12 school district in a nearby community. His background includes stints as a high school principal and an assistant superintendent. He also has held a variety of teaching posts, including some adjunct responsibilities in higher education.

The vacancy for the job of superintendent in Arcadia occurred after the hasty departure of the incumbent, who had been employed with the district for only two years. Abbey had heard about the opening and saw advertisements in professional publications. There was talk in some circles that Abbey was contacted by a member of the Arcadia school board and assured the job should he apply. Yet despite the rumors, a search process ensued. After screening and interviewing candidates, including a slate of three finalists, Abbey was selected as the front-runner and a representative group of board members visited his then-current district. Based on a vote of seven to zero in March, the board agreed that Abbey would be Arcadia's new superintendent, effective in July. Abbey was chosen primarily because he moves decisively after thoughtfully reflecting on the consequences, and he is able to elicit the best from his subordinates. With a low-key demeanor, he appears to value others in the decision making process.

The district seemed ready for a change in administrative leadership style, and Abbey was much different from his predecessor who operated in the "shoot from the hip" mode. Such a style served to keep the former superintendent in a defensive position when his decisions proved to be incorrect or volatile. For example, the previous superintendent had simply reacted to an issue involving race without fully considering the outcome when a faculty cheerleading sponsor was accused of unfairness in selecting cheerleaders. The superintendent publicly defended her without any kind of inquiry into the facts. Ultimately, the issue proved to be so explosive that the superintendent found himself standing before angry crowds of people who demanded an investigation. But it was not until after the situation was well out of hand, and included the involvement of local police to quell potential mob action, that the superintendent called for an investigation. Conducted by an independent third party, the investigation found that the sponsor had given favored treatment to certain students and had systematically excluded others. As it turned out, the students who were favored were white, and the excluded students were African American. Given this impartial report, the superintendent had to order new tryouts and promise a revised selection procedure in the future, using input from the community and safeguards to insure fairness.

The superintendent found himself in a no-win situation. The African-American parents were angry that he had to be forced to perform the duties of his job correctly. The white parents were angry that he acquiesced to pressure at the expense of white students, who in their opinion deserved to be cheerleaders. The teachers were angry that the superintendent did not stand by one of their members in a time of crisis. The school board was angry with the superintendent for embarrassing the school district.

Another example of an issue with sensitive racial overtones was the selection of the homecoming queen and her court. The concern centered on why, in a school district where the minority population is 40 percent, African Americans were never selected for the homecoming court. A similar defense of the status quo ensued and a retraction followed after the district was again in a near riotous state. The board was furious. Obviously these incidents were merely symptoms of a larger problem and the school board realized that it needed a leader with different skills.

As an outsider, Benjamin Abbey came in with a plan for getting to know the district and collecting data and opinions that would help him formulate an agenda for action. He was well received by the community and educators who seemed to appreciate his genuine willingness to listen and learn about them and their schools. Abbey emphasized that he brought with him no preconceived ideas other than to provide outstanding educational opportunities for pupils, parents, and patrons of the district. This approach offered an opportunity to heal old wounds, develop trust, and build on the strengths of people in the district. Abbey felt that the board members had already recognized that they were too deeply involved in the school district's day-to-day operations and personnel management. He worked closely with them to examine their roles and responsibilities in a board workshop soon after he started his job, focusing their activities more on policy and the big picture of the school district.

Three assistant superintendents were responsible for curriculum, personnel, and finance, respectively. One of the positions was vacant as Abbey arrived, which allowed him to select a new member of his senior staff. From those who applied, he chose a veteran insider. A retirement and a forced resignation permitted hiring two new principals. In both cases, Abbey promoted the most talented assistant principals from within the district. These moves won the respect of district insiders who saw that he valued loyalty, long service, and competence from existing administrative employees.

Within the first few days of his arrival, Abbey held a leadership development seminar for all administrators in the district. He defined the administrative team as including central office administrators and program directors, as well as building administrators at all levels. Early attention to staff development with the school board, the administrators, and later the teachers set the stage for Abbey's continued emphasis on personnel improvement and was one of the keys to his success.

The in-service staff development sessions in every case stressed human relations, race relations, community relations, and sensitivity training. Abbey brought in national experts in the field of human relations to lead various discussions. He even considered the need for the district to acknowledge its changing demographics, as well as openly signaling that business as usual would not be acceptable in the future.

The American Federation of Teachers represented the teachers as a bargaining unit. The teachers' organization at Arcadia had historically been friendly toward the administration, however due to the strained relationship with the previous superintendent, bridges had to be repaired. Abbey set out to systematically boost the trust and involvement of the teachers. One move he made was to promote a union officer to the position of assistant principal at one of the schools.

The prior administration's unilateral, reactionary style had damaged communications and trust to a great degree. Following his entry plan, Abbey made clear his commitment to communication, listening, rebuilding trust, seeking involvement, and providing a high-quality education system for the Arcadia school district. It was a concept he repeated at every opportunity. As a central part of his outreach, Abbey sent newsletters to every citizen in the school district, inviting them to volunteer and take part in all areas of the school system. He suggested that volunteers review all school district policies and procedures, and further asked citizens to participate in the budget planning process.

Signs of progress with Abbey's new approach to openness in the school district were apparent. Board members, meanwhile, were making strides of their own. Showing trust in the new district leader, the school board continued its strong support for the superintendent and his plans. To monitor the advancement of his program, Abbey used questionnaires and surveys to obtain feedback from the community, faculty, and students. In addition, he established a theme of communication, cooperation, and sharing with neighboring school districts. Within a short time, fellow superintendents viewed Abbey as a public relations leader.

The citizens' involvement committee, the budget committee, and the feedback structures were major elements in creating an atmosphere for change early on in the new superintendent's tenure. Key new hires in administrative posts helped to get things moving in a positive direction. And the training seminars and workshops for the school board and the administrators set the tone for leadership. At the end of his first year as Arcadia's superintendent, Abbey appeared to be well on his way toward achieving his goals. He had carefully followed the ideas and direction he had set forth on his arrival to the district, aligning his beliefs with the execution of his plan. He worked hard at establishing team spirit and open communications. Seeming comfortable in the job, with himself, and with the processes and structures he put in place, Abbey decentralized responsibility but kept his fingers on the district's pulse without becoming bogged down in details. A model of patience, he took time with all of his audiences to explain his and the district's views on total involvement, and why he felt it would make a difference. After a short time, confidence in the school system and district leadership was restored, thus allowing the district to go forward in educating all students without regard to their race or background.

As with many school districts that are in the first suburban ring surrounding a major city, it is not unusual to see districts like Arcadia coming to grips with the reality of new demographics, and a desire to employ a superintendent who will be sensitive to the diverse mix of students and citizens. The Arcadia school board had contemplated replacing their failed superintendent with one from a minority group since a number of similar districts were employing their first minority superintendent. Although Benjamin Abbey was not from a minority group himself, he was the right person for the Arcadia school district. His experience and wisdom proved to be a good fit for the school board and the community.

12

Barnet: Risky Politics

School district: Barnett—two high schools

Socioeconomics: Ranges from the working poor to middle-class

Demographics: About 2,400 students; 90 percent white

Superintendent: Dr. Earle Bacon—previously a principal in a nearby school district

The community of Barnet can be viewed as a Mayberry at the outer edge of a major metropolitan area. Although this historic, little river town is becoming a popular place where people move in search of refuge, Barnet still maintains its small town flavor. Typical of many modest communities, Barnet's 10,000 residents are basically conservative. So it's no surprise that the community, and thus the school district, takes pride in its thriftiness and lack of extravagance surrounding most undertakings. The core village still has the old street signs, not so much to maintain history but to avoid the cost of updating. The same is true of the old parking meters downtown, as well as the outdated storefronts that are reminiscent of a bygone era.

There is no identifiable large employer in Barnet. Like many small towns near larger communities, not even a hospital lies within the corporate limits. While the economics would indicate that Barnet is middle-class, some of the older residents are in conflict with the new, emerging prosperity. Thus, financially, the community represents two extremes: the very stable middle-class and the working poor. Many schoolteachers live in Barnet, and for the most part, are middle-class. Although some of the teachers who live in Barnet also teach in the school district, many of them are employed in neighboring districts. The most influential community groups in Barnet tied to the schools are band parents and the athletic boosters.

There are two high school campuses in the Barnet school district, both within the corporate limits of the village. One high school holds grades 9 and 10, and the other grades 11 and 12. The student populations of the two schools are 90 percent white, 7 percent African American, 2 percent Hispanic, and 1 percent Asian or other. The Barnet school district draws its students from six separate elementary districts that span roughly 70 square miles, some of them suburban, some rural. All of them are small kindergarten through grade eight districts that house from 300 to 1,000 students. Two of the districts have only one building, with the other four having from two to four buildings. Three of the six districts serve only white students. In two others, African American and Hispanic students make up 3 to 5 percent of the population. The remaining school district has a 90 percent ethnic minority student mix; 85 percent of the students are African American, and 5 percent are Hispanic.

Barnet is the kind of school town that many citizens yearn for—it's far enough removed from an urban environment and it has a rural feel. Yet along with that small town atmosphere comes small town behavior. While 26 percent of the students qualify for federally subsidized meals at school, most of the Barnet students and their parents tend to shun the students and families from a lower socioeconomic class. There is also noticeable racial bigotry present within the various communities feeding into Barnet, and therefore the Barnet school climate clearly reflects a caste system based on race and social class.

The bonding capacity for expanding the buildings and infrastructure in the Barnet district is near its limit, thus not allowing the kind of updating that is needed for the schools to keep pace with their growth. A recent increase in teachers' salaries following a strike has caused the district to run an annual deficit in its operating fund. If the district does not boost its revenue stream to keep pace with operating expenses it will have to drastically reduce expenditures. Such a reduction would greatly affect the quality of the education program and extracurricular activities. The only viable method available for increasing revenue in the Barnet district is a local ad valorem property tax rate hike. By state law, no new taxes can be levied without the approval of the voters living within the school district. Given the bitter feelings left in the community after the teachers' strike, coupled with the conservative nature of the town, it is unlikely that raising taxes will be supported unless the schools are viewed to be in dire straits.

The superintendent's position with the Barnet school district became vacant after the incumbent resigned at the end of his third year. Overall, district officials had been pleased with the incumbent's wisdom; he came to the district with organizational skills and the ability to work effectively, even with a climate of teacher and community unrest. Because the community leaned toward financial austerity, the superintendent often clashed with factions of the school board that were extreme in their views toward school financing. Late in the school year the superintendent announced his resignation to accept the superintendency of a larger school district in an adjacent state. With only a few weeks left before the start of the new school year, the board had few options for filling the position. They could initiate an official search, but given the short time frame, it would not likely yield a successful result. Most quality candidates had already landed new positions, and others who might be thinking about a move would probably defer their decisions until the following year. Another option was for the board to identify an interim superintendent and have that person serve until a proper search could be launched with a logical timeline. That would allow the district to advertise the opening during the normal school employment cycle and have a new superintendent start at a more appropriate time. But the board did not do either.

Thirty-nine-year-old Earle Bacon was a high school principal in a neighboring school district for three years when the Barnet vacancy occurred. Prior to his position as principal, Dr. Bacon worked in the Barnet school district as an assistant principal at one of the high schools. Although Bacon left Barnet for a neighboring district principalship, he and his family continued to live in Barnet. His children attended Barnet schools, and he was very active in the community as both a parent and a citizen. Due to his involvement in the village of Barnet and his prior knowledge of the school district as an employee, Bacon saw an opportunity in the superintendent's sudden departure.

With a doctorate from a major midwestern university, Bacon made it known that he was preparing to be a school superintendent. He had successfully taught and coached for several years prior to moving into school administration and was popular among residents of his school district as well as in the Barnet community where he lived. Bacon was even involved in organizations and activities that included some of the Barnet school district board members.

After a flurry of telephone calls and unofficial meetings between some of the Barnet school board members, the rumor began to circulate throughout the community that Bacon was being considered for the vacant superintendent's position. It appeared that news of Bacon's consideration was being floated as a trial balloon to test the reaction of the community and school staff. Sentiment was divided. There were people who were pleased that a person such as Bacon, considered an insider in some circles, was being mentioned for the top job. Some thought of Bacon as a known quantity who represented stability. Others were not in favor of Bacon, calling him a political opportunist attempting to obtain his first superintendency through the back door. One very negative comment was that Bacon had sought favor with four of the seven board members to appoint him without a formal search. Vocal critics cited Bacon's lack of experience as a superintendent—or even central office administrator—as a reason why he should not be considered. Still others had no objections to Bacon, only to the lack of a legitimate process. Several observers stated that it would be to Bacon's advantage to take part in a formal search process and surface as the favorite among school board members.

Because the district where Bacon worked was nearby, and he lived in the Barnet district, he felt he had kept abreast of important events in the Barnet schools. Paradoxically, Bacon believed himself to be both an insider and an outsider. He was an insider because he knew the district fairly well and was part of the political and social milieu of the Barnet community, yet he was an outsider because he was not employed by the school district. Bacon apparently saw no harm in exploring the possibility of his appointment, with support from only a faction of the school board. Never completing an actual application as traditional candidates for a superintendency are required to do, it was reported that Bacon was the only person to be interviewed by a committee of the board. Following the committee's interview, the board spent time debating as to whether Bacon's appointment was appropriate or even legal. Bacon was clearly favored by four of the board members who encouraged him to discuss contract provisions. Thus he moved ahead and negotiated a contract with a majority of four, and a meeting was set for his official appointment.

The notice for the board meeting to consider the employment of a new school superintendent was officially posted. The school auditorium was filled to capacity with citizens and staff who stood on both sides of the controversy. Before the vote took place, several people spoke up about the impending action. After an hour, the board voted four to three to end the public comment session and move on to the action for the evening. A motion and a second were made, with board discussion. Four board members favored the appointment and three objected. The roll was called and the board voted four to three to employ Earle Bacon as the Barnet district's superintendent of schools, with a two-year contract as stipulated by law for a person who has not previously served as a school superintendent. The announcement of the incumbent's departure and Bacon's appointment as Barnet's superintendent for the ensuing year took only 15 days.

Bacon believed that he could ultimately solidify the community behind his appointment. He also thought his knowledge and involvement would serve as a catalyst to bring the two factions of the board together to work in the best interest of the students. Bacon had his work cut out for him and he knew he had an uphill battle. His first order of business was to call for a meeting of all administrative staff and solicit their support as he prepared to move into the new position for the upcoming school year. He indicated that it was his desire to get to know everyone on the staff personally and that he wanted to hold social events on a regular basis so that administrators could become better acquainted. Bacon held the first of a series of administrative socials that spring while the incumbent superintendent was still in office. As a courtesy, he invited the incumbent, who graciously accepted. The social featured a party atmosphere and only fleeting references to school district matters. Given the fact that the current school year was winding down, little time was available to implement any other communication strategies in the school district. Bacon attended the final school board meeting of the incumbent superintendent's term as an observer and officially began his duties on the first day of July.

Bacon's initial action was to meet with the school board to work on establishing a relationship. He requested that board members join him for a private retreat to discuss exactly that, along with goals for the district. The majority of the board accepted the retreat idea; three members objected. As the board president and the superintendent planned the retreat, the three dissenters vowed not to participate. The retreat was held anyway, with the superintendent and four board members in attendance. At the retreat, the four board members pledged their support to the superintendent and expressed their confidence in his ability to lead the school district. However, the lines were once again drawn between the majority and those who openly opposed Bacon's appointment.

Bacon called for a districtwide faculty meeting to kick off the new school year. Given the fact that his appointment to the superintendency took place in the summer, this would be his first opportunity to meet with the entire faculty. With his informal style of speaking to groups, Bacon made his audience feel comfortable and he conveyed the impression that he was one of them. Except for a few notes that were needed to provide details of upcoming events and announcements, Bacon's address to the faculty was extemporaneous. He used humor to capture his audience and often laughed during his delivery. Ultimately, Bacon addressed the controversy of his unorthodox appointment. He stated that he was confident that he was the right person for the job and pledged to be a superintendent "for the people." He asked for staff support and declared his intentions to involve them in all important decisions that would affect their future.

In the ensuing weeks, Bacon met with various groups of employees as well as external constituents. A key internal group was the teachers' union. The union's reputation of militancy did not bother Bacon since he believed that the core leadership was one of his strongest supporters. Whether that was true or not, the union membership was not united behind Bacon: Some members openly expressed dissatisfaction with his appointment while others supported him unconditionally. Bacon's meeting with the teachers' union was cordial but tense. Again Bacon pledged to involve union leaders in all important decisions that pertained to them. Meetings with the other groups, such as the custodians, teacher's assistants, and cafeteria workers resulted in quiet compliance. Clearly there was an atmosphere of uneasiness throughout the school district.

Throughout the year, Bacon attempted to lift the cloud of doubt surrounding his appointment by pouring himself totally into his job. He was the first one in the office in the morning and the last to leave at night. On most weekends he could be seen either at his office or at school district sponsored events. Bacon continued to initiate social activities for the various groups in the district in an effort to allow people to get to know him better. But unfortunately, he developed a reputation as a "party person." Although some people liked the festive atmosphere that Bacon had created in the district others showed open resentment. And there were objections by some to alcohol being served at quasi official school functions.

Try as he might, Bacon was unable to mend his relationship with the dissenting board members. The same split that occurred at his appointment continued. Most issues requiring a direct recommendation from the superintendent were passed by the board on a four to three vote. The three board members voted against Bacon's initiatives and were vocal about their dissatisfaction with both his appointment and performance. They often called the news media and openly criticized the superintendent.

In the spring of the first year that Bacon was in office, a school board election was held. Four seats were open and Bacon's detractors held two of those seats. Bacon assisted his supporters on the board in identifying candidates who would back him as superintendent. His involvement was reported and editorialized by the media, and several citizens wrote negative letters to the editor. Bacon seemed unaffected by the criticism. In his opinion, it was entirely appropriate for the superintendent to be involved in any school board election that had the potential of changing the school district one way or another. The election concluded with Bacon's two incumbent supporters returning to the board, joined by one of their hand-picked candidates who defeated one of Bacon's detractors. The other detractor who was up for reelection was successful in retaining his seat. Moving into his second year, Bacon could now boast of having a five-member majority and only two members who opposed him.

Barnet's school board members had allowed themselves to fall into a trap of selecting a superintendent outside of a traditional selection process. Regardless of who contacted whom first, the employment of Earle Bacon was a blueprint for disaster. The school board was clearly accountable for bringing Bacon on board as superintendent under a cloud of suspicion. It was obvious, however, that Bacon enjoyed the intrigue.

Even though Bacon possessed some leadership skills, he started out on the wrong foot and continued to stumble throughout his employment at Barnet. His reputation as a reveler did not serve him well with many of the school district constituents either. Such behavior tends to plague superintendents as they move from district to district, and will ultimately reflect negatively on their reputation. Because of his volatile relationship with some board members, counting votes to get anything accomplished became a way of life for Bacon. To have to work in such an environment is far from ideal if a superintendent is to be effective.

13

Cambay: Harsh Fiscal Realities

School District:	Cambay—kindergarten through grade 8
Socioeconomics:	Average income is below poverty level
Demographics:	600 students, mostly minority
Superintendent:	Dr. Susan Cabot—previously principal in an adjoining district

Cambay is a small, rural school district nestled among suburban communities. The town is like many rural communities in appearance: Most streets are blacktopped, some remained unpaved, and there are no sidewalks. Cambay is an appendage to the larger village of Thornbird, which has repeatedly rejected requests by Cambay to be annexed. Annexation would give Cambay residents an opportunity to acquire city services such as sewer, water, and garbage collection. It would also provide the sidewalks and road maintenance many see as a necessity to improve the quality of life in Cambay. Still, a few of Cambay's citizens oppose annexation, citing the increased cost for services as not worth the investment. And there are some who actually prefer their rural existence and simply do not want to change.

Thornbird's citizens are similarly split on the issue of assimilating Cambay into their community. A quiet, mostly residential municipality of 10,000 residents, of which 99 percent are white, Thornbird boasts an average family income that places it solidly in middle-class, both economically and socially. Cambay, on the other hand, is 95 percent African American, many of its citizens are unemployed, and some households are headed by single parents or unmarried women.

It seems unlikely that Thornbird will ever accept Cambay as of part of its community through the official act of annexation, or even embrace or accept its residents as neighbors. The leaders and citizens of Thornbird flatly deny accusations of racism. Their rejection of Cambay merging with Thornbird is alleged to be based purely on the economics of annexing an area that is in such great need. They say it would be more advantageous to annex land or territory that is uninhabited and allow the village to develop at its own pace and within its financial means. The needs of Cambay are too great, they stress, and they rail at the possibility of bringing serious financial problems to the village of Thornbird. Proponents, however, argue that there would be no additional expense to Thornbird since Cambay residents would be taxed at a level that would pay for the added services and improvements. Naturally the counterargument is that too many Cambay residents are poor and unemployed and therefore cannot afford additional taxes.

While the debate continues with no resolution, one commonality that exists between the two communities is their high school district. That's the place where reality is confronted as Cambay students enter the ninth grade and mingle with students from five other predominantly white elementary districts that feed into a majority white high school located in the village of Thornbird. Prior to high school, Cambay students attend classes in their own elementary school district, where 90 percent live in poverty. One building contains kindergarten through third grade, a second building holds grades four through six, and a third building (referred to as the junior high), houses grades seven and eight.

The Cambay school board is comprised mainly of blue-collar, working class citizens, which is no surprise, given the fact that it is unlikely business professionals would choose to settle in a poverty-stricken environment such as Cambay. All seven board members—five men and two women—are African American. Three of the five men are employed and married with children. The other two men are employed, divorced, and have children. The two women are homemakers; one is a single parent of three children, and the other is a married mother of six.

Like many officials in small communities, Cambay's board members take their responsibility seriously and feel that they hold a position of great importance. While they may differ on some issues, the board members are united in their opinion that the school district should focus on improving student education. Yet how they go about demonstrating their passion for improving the school system varies greatly. Four of the board members strongly believe that the superintendent should administer the school system and that the board should perform as a governing body and hold the superintendent accountable. According to the other three board members, it is the board's responsibility to supervise the schools. They say it is totally within their scope to know and be involved in the administrative minutia of the school system, including day-to-day operations.

School board meetings last several hours, mainly due to the three board members publicly quizzing the superintendent on every detail of proposals that come before the board. Although the superintendent submits his recommendations with thorough written explanations several days in advance of the meetings, these board members ask questions, even if the answers are right in front of them. They also insist on reviewing expenses line by line, discussing them at public board meetings before any action is taken, and often request that items be removed from the list because they do not agree with the expenditures. Further, they refuse to acknowledge or accept the responsibility for reading and reviewing the bills prior to the meeting. The superintendent continually stresses that questions are always appropriate, but that they should be genuine.

The majority of the board members refuse to participate in the line by line questioning and constant badgering of the superintendent on every issue that comes before them. Most of the time they remain silent while the three nitpickers talk between themselves and to the superintendent. Rarely are a simple motion and a second followed by a vote without a long, protracted discussion. Very few citizens attend the meetings, which makes the board's behavior even more puzzling, since they are not playing to an audience. The district staff that does attend the meetings as part of their duties is immune to what has become the expected behavior of the three board members, and their eyes often glaze over. The superintendent remains patient and endures the torture, mostly because he knows that the majority of the board also deplores the situation.

The incumbent superintendent was beginning his fourth year in the position when he announced in October that he had been offered another superintendency and would be leaving the district in 30 days. Board members were confused and angered by the sudden announcement. They even checked with the school district's attorney to find out if the superintendent could be held to his contract, or at least be forced to stay until a time that his departure would be less disruptive to the school calendar. According to the attorney, the board could legally hold the superintendent to his contract, but advised against taking action to keep him in the district.

The untimely announcement of the superintendent leaving while under contract caused him to lose his strongest allies. His final month was very difficult as he faced a hostile staff, community, and school board. What kept up the superintendent's spirits in his last days in office was his belief that he was leaving for a better administrative assignment. Once the school board resigned itself to the fact that they would not challenge the superintendent's departure, they seemed to want him out as soon as possible. To reduce the tension, the board president suggested that the superintendent use his remaining vacation time to leave his job earlier, and the board would appoint an interim superintendent. There were no congratulations or farewell receptions offered as the superintendent approached his final days at the helm. The superintendent took the board president up on his offer to leave the post early and quietly disappeared from the district.

This traumatic event seemed to draw the factions of the board closer together. The majority of four and the minority of three began to have civil conversations. The discussions included the need to find an interim superintendent and review the procedure for hiring the superintendent's replacement. They agreed without much fanfare that the principal of the grade four through six building should become the interim superintendent, although they did not view him as a viable candidate for the superintendency. A temporary replacement from within the elementary building would act as principal until a new superintendent was employed. The school board, with the assistance of the interim superintendent and the board secretary, contacted the state's school boards association and requested that they conduct a search for a new superintendent. The board desired to have a new superintendent take over at the midpoint of the school year. The association agreed and the search began.

The school boards association posted a notice for the opening in several state and national publications. They also contacted promising candidates and sought nominations from respected individuals who could make qualified recommendations. Within a couple of months the association had identified three promising candidates and presented their credentials to the Cambay school board. After hearing a verbal summary of the candidates' experience, the school board scheduled a full day of touring the district and an evening interview with each one.

The board conducted the interviews over three successive days. At the conclusion, they agreed on a ranking. Their number one candidate outshone the two others, however their number two choice was also a strong contender. The candidate in the top spot was called and invited in for a final interview and contract discussions, but he indicated that he was no longer interested in the job. The board was disappointed yet not disheartened, since they had agreed that their second choice was also quite acceptable. However, their call to the second candidate also yielded a withdrawal. With the two front-runners out of the contest, the board notified the state school boards association that they were not interested in candidate number three, and the search would have to resume. While the board wanted a new superintendent to assume the position in the current school year, they reluctantly agreed that most serious candidates would likely come forth during a time more traditionally aligned with the school calendar.

Somewhere in their many discussions school board members agreed to contact Dr. Susan Cabot, the principal from the Thornbird high school that Cambay students attend after grade eight, and solicit her application. This particular principal had not applied for the position when it was posted and did not indicate that she had any interest in the job. The school board president was elected to call Cabot and ask if she would come in for an interview. Her answer was yes. A much-respected principal by the community and her staff, Cabot had been the head of the Thornbird high school for four years after serving as an assistant principal in a large, comprehensive high school in a neighboring community. Holding a doctoral degree from a respected university in the state, Cabot was viewed as a leader among her colleagues. A no-nonsense administrator who knew the business of school administration, she was considered to be a people person as well as an instructional leader. Although Cabot held the credentials, she had yet to apply for her first superintendency. But for her to become a superintendent would be no surprise to most who knew her. What was amazing, however, was the fact that she would consider her first superintendency in a district like Cambay, with its poverty and poor student achievement, and all the associated problems.

Once Cabot decided to take the offer seriously, she met with her superintendent to get his input. He advised against the move to Cambay and indicated that he himself would never consider accepting a position in a district with its profile. Such a decision, he said, would be detrimental to the career of any administrator who would take the job. Yet out of respect for Cabot, and in an effort to be supportive, he asked her to take a few days to think about the offer and then get back to him. As a precaution, the superintendent told the Thornbird school board that Cabot had been solicited for the vacancy at Cambay and was considering the position.

Cabot decided to accept the job and met with the board to negotiate the provisions of a contract that would take her from February to the end of June, at which time they would negotiate a new multiyear contract for the ensuing years. Upon learning of Cabot's impending departure from the

Thornbird high school, several citizens called and expressed their dismay, offering both their congratulations and condolences. Ultimately, the community sponsored a large farewell reception for Cabot and practically the entire village of Thornbird attended.

In her first day on the job, Cabot learned that the central office for the Cambay school district was comprised of herself and one secretary. The secretary was initially openly hostile toward Cabot, which made her job more difficult. Cabot eventually had to have a stern talk with the secretary about the need to be civil in such a small office. It was a culture shock to be working in an environment where there were so few people, but Cabot understood, given the district's size and need to spend conservatively.

Basically, Cabot was directly responsible for all of the traditional duties in a school district central office, such as business management, curriculum and instruction, human resources, and financial management. Arriving for work earlier than anyone else in the school district and staying longer gave Cabot time to review all of the written documents available to her in the office. She tried to contact the former superintendent to ask some questions, but he did not return her calls. She scheduled a transitional meeting with the interim superintendent that did not yield any substantive information. He also had applied for the superintendent's position but was not considered. Given the potential for bitterness, Cabot did not press him further.

Through her own digging and discussions with the secretary, Cabot learned that the school district was six months behind in paying bills. Although bills had been approved for payment by the school board and checks were written the next day, those checks were put into a drawer to wait until funds were available before mailing them out. The secretary explained that the previous superintendent had developed this ingenious system to mask the inadequate cash flow. Bills were paid based on true need, or payment was made to those who screamed the loudest or threatened to take legal action against the school district. In addition, he routinely struck deals with utility companies to make partial payments to maintain essential services.

Cambay's entire annual budget was $1 million and Cabot estimated the district was overspending by at least $200,000 per year. In researching the financial records she found no plans for a balanced budget. But Cabot did find that the budget submitted to the state was balanced by showing only the expenditures and not the encumbrances or the accumulated unpaid bills. Payroll was a priority and employees had always been paid on time, so no one suspected that the district was in a financial crisis. Cabot stopped short of quizzing the secretary and left unanswered the question of how much the interim superintendent knew about the financial crisis. In Cabot's own conversations with the interim superintendent, he had not suggested that there was a problem. If school board members had knowledge of the fiscal crisis, it was withheld during Cabot's preliminary discussion and formal interview with them.

Cabot decided to request a special meeting of the school board to reveal her findings. The board members were stunned beyond belief! Clearly they did not know about the serious financial irregularities. They did understand that money was always tight and expenditures had to be carefully scrutinized, but they were in the dark about the accumulated debt and unpaid bills. More than the fact of the crisis, they resented the coverup. Cabot was asked who else knew about the situation. She responded that only the secretary had acknowledged knowing about the problem; the interim superintendent gave no clues in any conversation to date.

The board wanted to quickly take action against the interim superintendent upon hearing Cabot's news. However they first needed to know officially if he was aware of the financial situation, citing that if Cabot could discover it in a few days, he certainly could have found out about it in the three months that he had served. And of course if he knew, why didn't he tell them? Cabot cautioned the board that discussions with administrative staff *below* the level of superintendent were her responsibility. The board deferred to her even though they did not agree, indicating that the transgression the interim made was as superintendent, not as a staff member, and therefore he was directly responsible to the board. Eventually Cabot convinced the board that she should be the one to confront the interim superintendent about his knowledge of the district's finances, and that's what she did.

Cabot called for a meeting with the interim superintendent the next morning and was very direct in her questioning. She simply asked if he knew about the financial mess. His response was affirmative, but he indicated that he did not know how to reveal the information to the school board. He stated that he was afraid of how they would react. Cabot needed to consider how she would approach the board and requested that the interim superintendent return to her office at the end of the day. He did, and submitted his letter of resignation. He did not want to suffer the public humiliation and embarrassment that this revelation would bring, preferring to leave the district immediately.

Cambay's financial crisis was now a public issue and Cabot scheduled a planning meeting with the school board to consider the district's options. The first choice was to ask the public for a tax rate increase so that the programs could be maintained while the district revamped its spending. The fallback position would be to reduce the budget by at least $300,000 to tackle the overexpenditures as well as to begin paying down the accumulated debt. A tax rate referendum was put before voters in early spring after a vigorous campaign on the part of supportive citizens groups, school district staff, and the school board. It failed by a narrow margin. Instead, the district would have to move forward with its backup plan to reduce expenditures for the ensuing year. After sharing information and seeking input from the community and staff, Cabot made her recommendations for budget cuts to the school board. They included: closing the kindergarten through grade three building and consolidating the student population; eliminating 10 teaching positions; letting two librarians go; getting by with five fewer teacher's assistants; increasing class size by an average of six students; cutting two custodial positions; and eliminating one secretarial position. As a final recommendation, Cabot indicated that she would leave the grade four through six principal's position unfilled and would absorb those duties herself. The board understood the gravity of the problem and voted to approve all of her recommendations without dissension.

Cabot pondered her future. She had come to a district located in a poor area mainly because she thought she could make a positive difference. While she was prepared for the sacrifices necessary to work with high-risk students and a community that lacked sophistication, Cabot was not prepared for the severe financial mismanagement that required her to all but dismantle the school district in order to survive. She decided that working in such conditions—with little hope for improvement—would not be something she was willing to endure long term.

Meeting with the school board in an executive session, Cabot shared with them her feelings about her future. She said she would not be seeking a multiyear contract as previously planned, but she would stay for the remainder of the school term while seeking a position in another district where she could find more professional and personal satisfaction. By the end of the school year, Cabot had a job offer to serve as assistant superintendent in a larger district. After serious contemplation, she stepped down from the superintendency at Cambay and accepted the new position for the upcoming school term.

A rural, poor school district, Cambay was fortunate in attracting a first-class superintendent in Dr. Susan Cabot. She came with instant credibility and performed at a high level during her brief stay in the position. Districts like Cambay too often make the mistake of failing to show the appropriate appreciation for their superintendent and lose them early in their tenure. The mistake is often realized too late, as was the case with Cabot. Cambay lost a highly-qualified individual. The misstep not only hurt the schools, but further tarnished the district's reputation, since most observers already viewed the district as a less than desirable place for a superintendent. Whether Cambay can attract another individual with skills and commitment equal to Cabot's remains to be seen.

14

Darwin: The Storm of Social Change

School District:	Darwin, kindergarten through grade 12
Socioeconomics:	Largely poor
Demographics:	33,000 students; 80 percent minority
Superintendent:	Dr. Charles Daley—served as associate superintendent in Darwin just prior to becoming superintendent; was an associate superintendent for instruction in another state

Darwin is a historic, urban city of 2,000 in the southeastern region of the United States. Holding on to tradition and shaped by remnants of the old South, this is a place where progress and history coexist. The skyline is attractive, with both vintage and modern buildings interspersed throughout the city. Planners have kept pace with the needs of a growing and thriving metropolis. The central core of the city is clean and attractive to residents and visitors alike. The older neighborhoods are well-maintained and there is little evidence of any problems on the surface. However Darwin, like any large urban center, does have an underbelly that few visitors to the city ever see. But the city has managed to keep substandard property to a minimum, and through strong code enforcement has been able to eliminate undesirable housing before it becomes concentrated or rampant.

African Americans seem to have always lived in Darwin. Like many parts of the South, Darwin participated in the legal separation of the races in its public schools. Up to and beyond the 1954 Supreme Court case of *Brown v. the Board of Education of Topeka*, Darwin had separate schools for whites and blacks. Following the court's decision to dismantle the segregated system, Darwin's school administrators responded like many southern vestiges of segregation: They took legal action in an effort to avoid the

Supreme Court order. They alleged that the order did not pertain to them, and they attempted to demonstrate that the schools, although separate, were equal and of high quality. A group of local citizens—mostly black community leaders—became plaintiffs against the school district's quest to maintain its status quo. While the battle by the school district was ultimately futile, the case lingered for nearly two decades, with token concessions on the part of the school district along the way. The school district even sought a compromise of partial desegregation, but that idea was soundly rejected by the plaintiffs. Eventually, after years of court battles, the judge issued a comprehensive final order to immediately remove all traces of segregation from the school district. The order covered student assignment, as well as employment and promotion within the school system.

The schools have struggled to make the transition from their dominance by the white middle-class. The segregation issue in the schools could not be separated from the segregation in the city itself as the two were so intertwined, like with so many cities in that part of the country. Specifically, the city council was responsible for approving the school district's budget. For this reason the city took an interest in most issues that confronted the school district. When turmoil erupted over the issue of desegregation, city fathers reflected the attitude of school district leaders.

An environment where whites and blacks once coexisted without violence became a hotbed of hostility and racial animosity. The schools were forcefully desegregated and the white middle-class—the majority at the time—began to leave the school district in droves. As an alternative to adhering to public school mandates regarding integration, they established private schools that only whites attended. Also, the rural areas around Darwin began to take on a suburban appearance as white families left the city and moved to the outskirts where blacks did not live. The Darwin school district became one where nearly 80 percent of the students were black; court ordered desegregation had left behind a student population that was largely poor and minority.

Although the district changed from a majority white student population to one that had a black majority, some school buildings still held a nearly 100 percent white student body while others were nearly 100 percent black. These practices of segregation within the system brought further protests and the court ordered that such practices cease. The solution required a large-scale busing program. Additional resentment followed, and more white students left the district.

The court order also addressed discrimination in employment and promotion within the school system. Blacks historically were not employed or promoted to the extent of their presence in the Darwin community and federal oversight brought a whole new attitude toward both. Not only were blacks to be given fair access to obtain leadership positions in Darwin's school system, such as principalships, but they were to have a chance to work at various levels of the school system, including the central office. The superintendent of the Darwin school district was white, as was the deputy superintendent. Black citizens took note of the fact that this overwhelmingly black school system had no black leaders at or near the top where the real decisions were being made, and serious public protests ensued.

The incumbent superintendent had been a part of the Darwin school system for nearly 40 years, 23 of those years as superintendent. He started as a teacher, and over time worked his way through the system and held many important administrative positions. He had been the principal of one of the highest achieving high schools in Darwin prior to ascending to the central office and eventually deputy superintendent. He was considered an understudy to the superintendent and the heir apparent to the top post. To become the superintendent of a segregated system and have to oversee the dismantling of that system was indeed a traumatic event. It was most difficult to be positive about desegregation when, in his opinion, an excellent school system was being destroyed and reconstituted as a mediocre system. As one of the primary opponents to desegregation, he spent nearly two decades fighting to maintain the school system that he once had known.

Even with the black student population making up 80 percent of the district's total, four of the seven members of the Darwin school board are white. The other three members are black, and are all well-respected, prominent citizens of the Darwin community. School board members in Darwin are appointed by Darwin's city council, also with a white majority, but the board operates as an independent body. Recommendations come from the superintendent, and actions are taken by the majority vote of the school board without advice and/or consent from the city council. It is only during the budget process that the school board must obtain council approval prior to final adoption. Capital building projects also require city council approval. However, the Darwin school district's day-to-day operation is left to the superintendent and his staff. The school board is well-trained and tends to defer to the superintendent, with minimal questioning, at public meetings. Those meetings actually seem so well-coordinated that some observers view them as staged.

After 21 years in office, the superintendent announced to the school board his intention to retire in two years. Talk centered on the process for finding a replacement. Although it had been a long time since a new superintendent was hired, there was a recollection of the procedure. This superintendent had been identified prior to the departure of his predecessor and was an understudy for a period of time before assuming the top position. The board members decided that they wanted to continue that tradition and have a successor come aboard while the incumbent superintendent was still employed by the school district.

The school board secured the services of a superintendent search firm and launched a six-month nationwide search for the new Darwin superintendent. Board members got along well together during the search process, talking freely about the needs of the school district and generally agreeing on most important matters. One issue they addressed was the possibility of attracting a highly-qualified, black superintendent. While the advertisement did not specify a racial preference, the board desired to hire a black superintendent. They were aware of other successful black superintendents serving in positions throughout the country. Yet they were told very quickly by the consultants that attempting to lure a practicing superintendent to become an understudy with the hope of becoming Darwin's superintendent was a tough sell. Most successful superintendents would not see the job in Darwin as a promotion, or would not want to gamble on the likelihood that the school board would follow through on its implied promise. To avoid the issue of convincing a practicing superintendent to step down to come to Darwin, the board instructed the consultants to search for highly successful deputy or associate superintendents who would see the move to Darwin, and ultimately the superintendency, as less of a risk. Again, the board was interested only in qualified candidates, but made it clear that the Darwin community would be well served if the next school superintendent were black.

Dr. Charles Daley was serving as an associate superintendent for instruction at a mid-sized urban school system in the western region of the United States. At age 37, he was a bright and rising star among school administrators. He had successfully served as a teacher, principal, and central office administrator in three different school systems. His reputation as a highly-qualified school leader was even further elevated when he was selected, along with others, to advise the United States Office of Education on matters pertaining to improving the quality of urban education. In his own district, Daley was considered the likely choice for superintendent when the position became vacant.

Daley heard about the impending vacancy in the Darwin school district and was curious enough to seek more information. After a few contacts within unofficial networks around the country, he decided to officially inquire about the opening through the consultants retained by the Darwin school board. The consultants were extremely pleased to learn of Daley's interest. In their opinion, Daley was just what the school board had ordered. The official search continued, with several promising candidates surfacing through the process. But Daley remained a strong candidate in a field of outstanding applicants. His goal was to become a superintendent in a mid-sized urban school system and his preparation and experiences were geared toward one day moving into that position. Daley knew that it was possible to move up in his current district, but he was not willing to wait the five or six years for the incumbent to retire. So the Darwin school system seemed like a viable alternative to achieve his goal.

The consultants culled the applicants down to their recommended six best candidates, including Daley, and met with the school board to narrow the field down to the final three. Daley of course Daley remained among the board's three finalists. In their interviews, the board stressed to the candidates that they were searching for a superintendent who was willing to serve in the position of associate superintendent for two years before moving officially into the superintendency. The board was drawn to Daley; the youthful, accomplished administrator was very mature and wise beyond his years. After two interviews and a visit to the site of his potential employer, Daley was offered the position of associate superintendent at Darwin and he accepted. Daley was to serve for two years beginning July 1, and with a successful tenure, would be elevated to the superintendency upon the retirement of the incumbent superintendent.

Daley was the perfect understudy. He was careful in his relationship with the superintendent, finding it advantageous to defer to the incumbent rather than imposing in matters that might highlight the differences between them. He also realized that it would be important to get along with his superior, who still wielded a great deal of political clout within the school system and the city. Daley had a keen sense that if negative comments were made about him by the superintendent to certain people within the city of Darwin and the school district, it could be detrimental to his future. The school board sensed similar pressure and exercised caution in their relationship with Daley; they were very courteous to him but continued to give due respect to the superintendent.

The incumbent served as an able teacher and enjoyed his final 18 months free from acrimony. The school board was pleased with the relationship between Daley and the superintendent. During those months, Daley developed a reputation as a serious educator and leader. As associate superintendent he was responsible for overseeing and implementing the instructional programs of the school district. One of his greatest challenges was working with the deputy superintendent, who was in charge of day-to-day system operations. While the deputy was considered to be the closest to the superintendent, it appeared that he never assumed that he would, nor did he desire to be considered to take over the superintendency upon the incumbent's retirement.

Daley proved to be the right transitional administrator for a system that had no history with leaders of color at or near the top of the organization. His temperament was such that some described him as aloof. He showed no favoritism toward whites or blacks within the system and displayed by his deportment that he could work with all people, regardless of race. Thus, it did not take long for most observers to see the wisdom of the school board and the inevitability of Charles Daley as the next superintendent of schools for Darwin.

In the month of May, and within 60 days of the incumbent superintendent's official retirement, the school board took action to appoint Daley as its next superintendent, effective July 1. The leaders of Darwin, as well as internal and external school system observers, seemed pleased with the selection. Daley was grateful, but graciously waited until the departure of the incumbent before making any strategic statements about the district under his leadership. Following the July 1 effective date, he requested a two-day retreat with the school board for the purpose of establishing their future working relationship. The board accepted; they would meet with their new superintendent within two weeks, at a location 50 miles from the school district. The president of the board and the superintendent met to plan the structure and content of the retreat. It was decided that no one other than the superintendent and the board members were to attend, and the minutes of the meeting would not be made available to the public.

During the first day of the retreat, the new superintendent shared with the school board his detailed observations of the school system.

- He described a system that was deeply divided racially, and one that needed much healing.
- He revealed what he saw as "inappropriate connections" between certain members of the current school district leadership staff and persons who were involved politically with city council members.
- He felt that discussions that were considered confidential prior to the need to go public were often compromised.
- He said that he was aware of several school principals who were ineffective in performing their duties and needed to be replaced if progress was to occur.
- He discussed his desire to have a smaller, inner circle of school leaders who would interact along with him in future communication with the school board.
- He expressed his concern that some high-level administrators would have difficulty transferring their loyalty from the previous superintendent to the new administration.

Daley further stressed that a system with an 80 percent ethnic minority in its student population and community should have a staff that is more reflective of those groups. He concluded by stating that his success would depend on complete support from the school board in making appropriate changes to improve the system.

On the second day, school board members responded to points made by the new superintendent. They acknowledged all of Daley's observations as valid, and stated that they too were aware of the breaches of confidence from within the current administration. They added that the previous administration appeared not to care to take corrective action or remove incompetent administrators. In addition, they supported Daley's contention that the system was seriously out of balance regarding minority leadership at various levels. At the end of the second day, the school board pledged its support for the new superintendent and urged him to reorganize the administration in whatever way he felt was necessary to achieve success with the system.

The following week Daley met with the deputy superintendent, who had held that position under the former superintendent for five years, and established the ground rules under which the deputy would maintain his position. In the two years Daley and the deputy superintendent had worked together, they developed a rapport and genuine respect for one another. Daley believed that the cooperation he received from the deputy was due in part to the deputy realizing that Daley would one day be the superintendent and it was wise to be supportive. Nevertheless, Daley decided that it would be politically smart to keep at least one high-level administrator from the past administration to balance the reaction he anticipated to his agenda for district reorganization.

Throughout the next month, Daley met with the deputy superintendent to craft a plan to reorganize the administration from top to bottom. The planning featured a study of administrative structures in other mid-sized urban school districts across the county. The salient goal was to develop an administrative system that would streamline the delivery of educational services to the classroom, as well as increase accountability for performance by all of those involved in leadership positions. Ultimately, Daley intended to put together a team that would understand the shift in how school district business would be conducted in the future.

After two months had passed, Daley held a press conference—flanked by the school board and the deputy superintendent—and announced the new administrative structure for the school system. It would be implemented over the course of the current school year. In addition to declaring all central office administrative positions vacant, he announced that there would be a rotation and/or elimination of administrators at the building level. The new organizational chart was published for all to see, followed by a posting of the positions that were needed under the reorganization.

The internal reaction to the new organizational structure was mixed. Many people who believed the past system was open only to the well-connected sighed with hope that fairness in appointments would follow. But some long-term administrators attempted to marshal support to overthrow the plan, citing that the reorganization was designed to root certain people out of the system. The new superintendent was unyielding and the school board stood firmly behind him. The deputy superintendent served as a neutralizing agent when certain white administrators accused the new superintendent of actions that were racially motivated in his removal of long-serving white administrators. Eventually the school board, the city council, and the local news media applauded the new superintendent's courage in taking the initiative to restructure the school system, which was something that was long overdue.

By midyear, Daley had met with all the administrators who would be displaced and invited them to compete for the opportunity to serve in the new organization. Postings for the positions brought applicants from within and outside the Darwin school district. To deal with the magnitude of the screening and interviewing process, Daley put together teams made up of external experts for the positions under review. The various panels were chaired by the deputy superintendent and worked throughout the year to bring the top finalist for each position to Daley. He selected about 25 percent of the existing central office administrators to fill the reconstituted positions, and promoted another 25 percent from building level jobs to positions in the central office. The remaining 50 percent of the positions were filled by individuals from outside of the school system, many of whom came from urban school districts in other states. Individuals who were displaced either retired or were reassigned to lower level positions, including teaching assignments. At the building level, 30 percent of the principals maintained their current assignments. With the deputy's help, the superintendent rotated 50 percent of the principals to different buildings and reassigned the remaining 20 percent to lower level positions. Several building level administrators opted to leave the system rather than accept lower reassignment. Vacancies that were left after the shuffling and resignations were filled by internally promoted assistant principals and applicants from outside the district.

Throughout the year of rebuilding, Daley met with internal and external constituents in a planned series of "get acquainted" meetings. The meetings included the employee unions, as well as parent-teacher associations. Daley made his rounds of the civic, business, and social organizations, and the clergy throughout the school community, and made his case for organizational reform. In reflecting with the school board at the end of the first year, it was noted that the new administration had set in motion an organization that would move the system forward and establish the order for accountability for all leaders. Accolades for a job well done came from various sectors of the school system and the community, hailing Charles Daley for his vision and fortitude. Daley was well on his way to leading the school district in becoming a dynamic learning community that recognized all people as having dignity and worth.

Darwin is like many mid-urban school districts that have spent a great deal of time and resources resisting a desegregation order by the federal courts. Even during contemporary times, the district held on to outdated traditions that effectively excluded minority students from obtaining equal access to education programs in the school system. Despite the school board acknowledging a desire to attract a successful, black superintendent, there were lingering doubts about losing power and control. But the district's positive experience with Charles Daley, a no-nonsense school leader and a pioneer, helped bridge attitudes from the old ideas to the progressive ways of the future.

15

Epirus: A Balancing Act

School District:	Epirus—three high schools
Socioeconomics:	Middle-class and low-income blue-collar
Demographics:	6,000 students of diverse racial and ethnic backgrounds
Superintendent:	Diane Ellis—formerly an Epirus administrator and an assistant superintendent in another state

Epirus is a city of 90,000 that is racially, ethnically, and economically diverse. Yet it is a city in transition—from the historically proud, old, Victorian community it once was, to one that is made up of predominantly blue-collar, working-class residents who have lived there for the last 20 years. In its heyday, Epirus had a thriving downtown and was the beacon for all towns within a 50-mile radius. Epirus, like many cities of its era, hung on to the past, while other communities changed with the times and accepted shopping malls and other developments as a new way of life. The demise of the downtown and the loss of shopping traffic have left some vacant and unkept buildings in the city's landscape. Over time, many of the wealthy residents sought refuge in more progressive communities. But the city's solid support from industry, along with a community college and two private universities, has helped keep the economy viable and maintain a core of middle-class residents. Those who continue to live in Epirus are either loyal to their city or without adequate financial resources to move elsewhere. And as new residents arrive, they bring with them a lack of appreciation for what Epirus has meant to the region.

The school district, like the community, was once considered a beacon for educational excellence in the region. And although the three large comprehensive high schools in Epirus are still viewed to be excellent schools, they have experienced a recent decline in enrollment. Student demographics among the high schools have changed a bit over the last three years—from

95 percent white, to a still relatively balanced mix of 80 percent white, 15 percent African American, and 5 percent Hispanic. Yet the shift has made some white families uncomfortable, and they have opted to leave the district rather than have their children attend school with a growing minority population. Their departure is inciting others to leave, and further altering the district's demographics.

However, despite the changing economic climate that has brought in students of different racial and ethnic backgrounds, the district has maintained its pride and held on to its historic reputation. It is a reputation that actually prompts some parents to seek opportunities to send their children to Epirus schools, even if they live outside district boundaries. Epirus remains an award winning school district in the area of performing arts and athletics; that did not change even as the population became more diverse. Epirus students also perform well academically, and teachers continue to regard Epirus as a good place to live and advance their careers. Indeed, the superintendents of the five elementary districts that feed students into the Epirus high schools all see the Epirus superintendency as the prize among the school leadership positions in the area. Typical for the leadership positions at the high school level in this part of the country, the superintendent of Epirus, by stature of the district, enjoys a great deal of respect from others across the region and the state.

Epirus's superintendent, in the meantime, was creating quite a reputation of his own. The Epirus school board was so fed up with him that they decided not to renew his two-year contract. In a very short time, he had managed to alienate almost every sector of the school community, as well as members of the board, and they couldn't risk more damage. The search for a new superintendent was just beginning when Diane Ellis, a talented, 35-year-old administrator, serving in her second year as an assistant superintendent for educational services in a mid-sized school district in another state, heard of the opening in Epirus. Previously, Ellis was assistant superintendent for human resources in the Epirus school district. She had been invited to come to Epirus by the superintendent of schools, and during her employment in the district she enjoyed tremendous popularity with all sectors of the internal and external publics. Near the end of his second year in the position, the superintendent who brought Ellis to Epirus announced that he would be leaving to take a job as superintendent in another state. Thus, the Epirus school board began a national search for a new superintendent, and the board president encouraged Ellis to apply for the position. Her goal was to be a superintendent one day, but she was surprised by the overture. After much soul searching and consultation with family members and trusted colleagues, Ellis accepted the board's invitation to apply.

The school board narrowed the applicant field to three finalists, including Ellis, after interviewing six. Final interviews followed, with the school board selecting a candidate who was a superintendent in another state. Ellis was not remorseful but instead appreciative of the opportunity to be viewed as a viable candidate. She later learned that most board members looked upon her favorably, yet were reluctant to support her due to her role as an administrator in human resources rather than education. It was rumored that the board felt human resource administration was too far removed from the real duties of a district superintendent; they thought the best candidates had to come from the educational side of the administrative structure. After hearing about the school board's comments, Ellis contemplated the damage to her career that would result from being typecast as a human resource specialist. Even though it was late in the hiring season, she decided to pursue a position as an assistant superintendent for educational services. Within a few weeks and following a couple of interviews, Ellis was offered such an opportunity in a school district out of state, just prior to the official arrival of the new superintendent in Epirus.

When the new superintendent arrived, he spent time conversing with each of the assistant superintendents to ascertain how their positions functioned within the organization. In his meeting with Ellis, she revealed that she had been offered a position out of state and would be requesting a release from her contract with Epirus. The superintendent surprised her by indicating that it was inappropriate for her leave without giving a 60-day notice. Ellis had never heard of such a requirement, but respected the wishes of the superintendent. She said she would then stay at Epirus since she was certain that her new employer would not be willing to wait the 60 days for her to begin. Her decision pleased the new superintendent. Ellis also telephoned the out-of-state district to inform them that she had been refused release and regretted not being able to make the move. She did mention the 60-day notice, but felt it would be unfair to her new employer. Two days later, Ellis received a call from the out-of-state superintendent who indicated that he had spoken with his school board and relayed the events and the dilemma that caused her to turn down the position. His conversation included comments regarding the great respect he and the board had for Ellis related to the sacrifice she was making for the new superintendent in Epirus. He added that both he and the board would be pleased to have her join their district staff after the 60 days her superintendent demanded.

Ellis requested a meeting with the new Epirus superintendent to relay the turn of events. The superintendent was disappointed, but acknowledging that she had met his conditions, agreed that she could leave her job at Epirus after 60 days. Ellis spent that time creating the most positive atmosphere that she could. She spent countless hours assisting the new superintendent in his transition and even helped him identify the best prepared person from within the staff to succeed her. The superintendent was very grateful and thanked Ellis for her support as she left Epirus and reported to her new district 60 days later.

Ellis excelled in her new position, even though she had to play catch-up from starting so late in the school year. The superintendent in the out-of-state district had prepared the staff to welcome her as a talented leader with an outstanding track record. She took to the new position quickly and the staff members with whom she worked, along with the superintendent, were very impressed. Ellis intended to stay in the district for a reasonable period of time so that she could benefit from the leadership skills that came with being an assistant superintendent for educational services. She thoroughly enjoyed her job and envisioned continuing in it until the right opportunity for a superintendency became available.

After about 15 months, Ellis received a telephone call at her home from the president of the Epirus school board. The conversation began with an inquiry as to how Ellis was doing in her new job, in addition to small talk. Ellis was cordial but confused as to the purpose of the call. However that was made clear when the president asked how she felt about the possibility of coming back to Epirus as the superintendent. Startled by the question, Ellis managed to respond that she was not aware that the position was vacant. The president acknowledged that it was not, but the majority of the school board was extremely dissatisfied with the performance of the superintendent. Ellis told the board president that she was uncomfortable with the conversation, and with all due respect, she had no interest in discussing the possibility of becoming the district's superintendent of schools when there was no official vacancy. With that comment the conversation ended, and both said their polite good-byes.

Four months later Ellis received another call from the Epirus school board president. This time he avoided preliminary conversation and went right to the reason for his call. He began by reminding Ellis of what she had said when he asked about her interest in the superintendency during their last conversation. Then he restated her words expressing a lack of interest in a superintendency where there was no vacancy. Ellis responded that his recollection was correct. That's when the board president told Ellis that based on the board's action the previous evening, the Epirus school board would not be renewing the superintendent's contract. There were, however, four board members prepared to hire Ellis as the new superintendent. Ellis was again startled, yet managed to say that she did not want to give the impression that her interest was contingent on the board vacating the position for her. The board president assured her such was not the case; the superintendent's firing was inevitable. Nevertheless, Ellis suggested that the president allow her a few days before responding.

After one week, Ellis phoned the board president with several questions. Her first was to ascertain what authority the board president had to call and offer her the job. He responded that the majority of the board had commissioned him to make the call, and that the other three board members had not been consulted but surely would be pleased if they learned of her interest. If they did not go along, he continued, it would not matter, since the board clearly had enough votes to bring her in as superintendent. Anticipating the possibility of this response, Ellis was prepared with her answer. She said that she had fond and positive memories of Epirus and was flattered by the prospect of returning to the district as the superintendent, however she was not comfortable with anything that gave the appearance of illegitimacy. Ellis asked the board president to convey the message that she was not interested in the job at this time, given the circumstances of what appeared to be a clandestine coup. She suggested the board post the job through the normal process without consideration of her as a candidate. The telephone call ended with the board president saying he understood Ellis's position and appreciated her integrity.

Ellis immersed herself in her job and watched for news of the Epirus vacancy. Within a few weeks the posting was circulated via the national sources that were typically used to advertise for a superintendent of schools. She noted the job description and duties, along with the deadline for applying. Ellis privately acknowledged her interest in the Epirus superintendency and wished she had not gotten caught in the middle of the attempted recruitment without a proper process. After several sleepless nights, Ellis decided to consult with her family and trusted colleagues about her dilemma. The feedback verified that she had handled the situation correctly; the advice she received about how to proceed mirrored her own thoughts. Ellis would apply for the position within the stated deadline and make no contact with the school board other than through her official application. She wanted her credentials to stand on their own merits and not be tainted by the kind of politics that caused her to reject the overture from the board president. Ellis prepared her application packet with the kind of care required of a good candidate and submitted it to the school board through the professional search firm that was retained to identify superintendent candidates for Epirus.

The consultants completed the process of winnowing down the applicants and gave their report to the school board in a closed session. As part of their presentation, they described the eight strongest applicants from the field of 60 who had applied. The session was designed so that the consultants could recommend a broad group from which the board would select three. The process took about three hours and board members took their responsibility very seriously. They were surprised to see the application from Ellis, but made no comments as they went about their task. By the end of the evening, the board had narrowed the field to three candidates, which included Ellis. The next step was for the consultants to contact the successful finalists on behalf of the board and set up interviews.

Ellis was pleased to receive the call from the consultants, who also relayed their observations of the board's behavior upon learning of her application; the reaction was positive, but one of surprise. Ellis's chances of securing the appointment were strong, added the consultants, based on the board's discussion. She was given the opportunity to choose an interview slot first, since she would be coming from the greatest distance. Ellis chose the last slot. She arrived for the interview a few hours early and drove around the school district to get a feel for any changes that might have occurred during the two years she had been away. She went to the local newspaper and reviewed two years of back issues to find out what kind of news had been reported about the school system. She learned that the tenure of the previous superintendent had been tumultuous and fraught with controversy—between him and almost every sector of the school community. He also had several public clashes with members of the school board.

At the interview, Ellis was greeted politely by the board president, who escorted her to the room where the other board members were waiting. The session commenced with the pre-established questions being read by individual board members. With a formal but relaxed atmosphere, the board members appeared to treat Ellis as a person they had known for years, and with whom they could share conversations about the school district. After about an hour, the formal questioning was completed, however the board did not dismiss her. Instead, they sat around and chatted for another hour. They all seemed very much at ease, even Ellis. The board president told Ellis that a decision would be made in about a week, and the consultants would contact each finalist regarding the outcome. At that time the successful candidate would be informed of the next steps, including the possibility of board members visiting the finalist's home district.

Eight days after the interview, Ellis received a call from the consultants. She had been selected as the finalist by the board in a closed meeting held the previous evening. Deliberations lasted less than 30 minutes, said the consultants' representative, with all of the board members quickly agreeing that Ellis was the best choice for the job. Their time was spent discussing whether Ellis was a serious candidate, and whether she would actually come back to Epirus. Further, the board was not interested in conducting a site visit since they felt Ellis was someone they already knew. The board was ready to negotiate a contractual agreement if Ellis was also ready. Ellis was elated and immediately accepted the offer to negotiate. After meeting with her attorney and receiving guidance, she set a date with the school board through their consultants. Following successful negotiations with the board, Ellis was appointed superintendent of schools for the Epirus school district effective July 1.

Upon reporting to the district to begin her duties, Ellis requested a meeting with the board president. In their meeting, Ellis expressed her delight at being appointed superintendent and set forth her ideas for what she believed should take place prior to the start of the new school year.
During the course of the conversation, Ellis broached the topic of the discussions she had with the board president prior to her decision to apply for the superintendency. She felt she owed him an explanation as to why she decided to submit an application without recontacting him first. The pres-

ident was both relieved and grateful that Ellis was addressing the issue. He thanked her and assured her that no explanation was necessary. He said he respected her for the decision she made, and that the majority of the board who knew of the earlier proposal respected her. According to the board president, Ellis was the clear favorite of all the board members, and he was glad that she had decided to return to the district through the front door. Ellis said she preferred not to know the identity of the other three board members who were a party to the earlier plan. The board president honored her request, and the subject was never raised again throughout her association with the Epirus school district.

Ellis began her work at Epirus with a school board retreat, wherein she and board members together outlined the challenges facing the district. Ellis shared with the board her observations of the district and her thoughts about the healing that was needed following the events of the past couple of years. She cited her personal approach to communication and her desire to spend a great deal of time listening to the various constituent groups. She insisted that board members outline what they expected of her during the course of the upcoming year. The board, with Ellis's participation, went through an exercise to identify achievable goals for their new superintendent. Those goals were then turned into a written document and attached as an addendum to her contract.

Following her retreat with the school board, Ellis sent letters introducing herself to all the major groups within the school community. In her letters, she offered to meet with each group for the purpose of getting acquainted. After the school year resumed in the fall, Ellis scheduled meetings with all of the internal groups within the school district. Some groups, such as unions, were formally structured, while others were recognized only by what the members had in common, or the kind of work they performed for the district. Regardless, Ellis spent time with all classes of employees. She also gave special attention to her administrative staff, by hosting a special, full-day retreat so that they could get to know her better. Needless to say, Ellis was well received by all groups and lauded for her willingness to be open and listen to their concerns. The healing process was underway for a school system that had experienced a very traumatic two years. Diane Ellis was the kind of superintendent that the district needed to move forward and once again place it in a positive light with the citizens of Epirus. Moreover, board members were glad that they were able to attract a professional with such high integrity.

Epirus is a study in how a school district passed over a highly qualified insider to employ an outsider who was basically ineffective for the two years he held the position. It is possible that the outsider's lack of success was due to some board members feeling that the insider, Diane Ellis, should have been selected as the superintendent instead. Ellis accepted a position as assistant superintendent in another state, yet her departure was executed with a great deal of class. Some individuals in similar situations would have felt animosity toward the board, but not Ellis. She left the district on a very positive note, without rancor or an unkind word. Her attitude toward the Epirus superintendency was that it obviously was not meant to be, and there was no reason to be bitter. She wished everyone well, including the new superintendent.

The fact that the school board sought her out within two years amazed her. Instead of simply accepting their invitation, she contemplated whether or not to apply through a legitimate process or to pass on the opportunity altogether. When she eventually did apply, it was without the cloud of conspiring with board members to obtain the job in a noncompetitive manner. The school board respected her integrity, which had a significant impact on her relationship with board members throughout her tenure.

16

Finley: Mediawise Superintendent

School District:	Finley—kindergarten through grade 12
Socioeconomics:	Largely working class
Demographics:	15,000 students; 15 percent minority
Superintendent:	Lamont Fitch—previously a superintendent in another state

Located in the Midwest, Finley is a stable, urban community with the potential for additional growth due to available adjacent land and the recent annexation of unincorporated areas. With a population of 150,000, this largely working class city has a private university, a community college, and two regional hospitals. As a capital city, it also houses all state agencies and employs thousands of people, many of whom live in Finley solely because of their employment with the state.

Finley public schools only educate students who live within the Finley corporate limits, and as new territory is annexed to the city, the school district grows. The district has three high schools, five middle schools, and 27 elementary schools. Eighty-five percent of the students are white, 10 percent are African American, and 5 percent are Hispanic or Asian. Twenty percent of the students are eligible for the free lunch program. Although the Finley school district and community are proud of having small school populations and class sizes, the district struggles to convince the middle class to stay in Finley's schools and not flee to suburban districts.

The school district's central office sits at the edge of downtown. In addition to the superintendent, the central office consists of three assistant superintendents and 35 other administrators. The seven-member Finley school board is made up of six professional people—a medical doctor, a banker, a social worker, two college professors, a businesswoman—and a homemaker. The board wanted a superintendent who would bring about community cohesiveness, as well as improve Finley's schools. Instead, they recently completed the buyout of the incumbent superintendent's contract after he proposed a controversial school closing plan that met universal rejection. Even after the school board voiced concerns that the plan was ill-fated and would not be acceptable to the community, the superintendent continued his sales pitch with reckless resolve. Losing confidence in their superintendent, the school board negotiated his departure, but not before a very difficult period in which the public also lowered their opinion of the school system.

Another wound—one that had festered in the Finley school district for more than a decade—was the open breach between labor and management. Negotiations between the teachers and the school board stalled every year. Binding arbitration became the rule, and each negotiation session was heated. Both sides of the bargaining table had a history of poor relationships and neither were willing to compromise to end the hostility. A big part of the problem, according to the teachers, was the attorney who acted as the board's chief negotiator. The teachers saw the attorney as an outsider insensitive to their needs. They pleaded for the board to bring new leadership to the bargaining table—leadership that understood the big picture of professional K-12 education. Collective bargaining, as viewed by most observers, was a collective failure.

Finley's search for a new superintendent yielded four outstanding candidates, one of which was Lamont Fitch. Two of the candidates were from the state and held solid reputations as school leaders, while Fitch and the fourth candidate were from out of state. Fitch, a 41-year-old white male and Tennessee native, settled in the Midwest after graduating with a degree in mathematics from an academically elite, liberal arts university. He taught in a large, metropolitan district before entering administration as an assistant principal. A high school principalship followed, and then a stint as an assistant superintendent. Fitch had been a superintendent of schools for five years when the search consultants contacted him about the opportunity at Finley.

Despite having been very successful as the superintendent of a district with 6,500 students, Fitch had a personal desire to move on to a larger urban district. He wanted to make a positive impact on a school district that needed help in achieving a higher standard. At the time the search consultants contacted Fitch, he had interviewed for four superintendencies within his own state. He was already the front-runner for three of the positions. But Fitch put off making any decision about those superintendencies to consider the possibility of the top job in Finley.

After interviewing the first three candidates, the Finley school board was split over which of them would be most suitable for Finley, and they had not yet interviewed Fitch. The board had agreed before the interviews that each candidate would be discussed in closed session immediately following their interview, and a final discussion would be held after the four interviews were concluded. In that final discussion, the first candidate to receive support by the majority of the board would be offered the position. By the time the board had interviewed three of the candidates, it was difficult to resist making comparisons. They were very impressed with the qualifications and began to make a pitch for their favorite. Convinced that the new superintendent was among the first three candidates interviewed, the board members began polling each other.

Had the majority of four supported one candidate, the board agreed that they would end the search and notify Fitch that there was no need for him to come in for his interview. The informal poll revealed that three board members favored the first candidate, three favored the second, and one favored the third. They recognized the deadlock and agreed that it was premature to be lining up behind candidates before interviewing the fourth finalist.

Fitch was prepared and polished during his interview with the board. The opening question allowed him to demonstrate his ability to articulate his past experiences and successes. In the fashion of a take-charge leader, Fitch elaborated upon each answer and concluded with a direct reference to Finley. He was able to pinpoint specifics regarding issues within the school district and the community. He even brought charts and graphs to show the board the progress made in the school district under his superintendency, and cited his ability to work with the media to publicize favorable information about the school system. He ended his interview with a structured game plan for improving the Finley school district and added that the public would not take notice unless the district also had a strategy for telling its story.

Fitch's ability to make statements related to the needs of Finley's school system came partially as the result of the two days he spent in the district prior to his interview. Before his visit, he gathered all the data that were available via sources such as the Internet and past news reports. Then he made telephone calls and asked questions of various constituents. Fitch used his trip to Finley to verify his initial findings about the school district and collect more information. He certainly was enthused about the potential to make a difference in Finley, and saw the district's size as an advantage over the smaller district and community of his own superintendency: Finley was large enough to support the level of staff assistance needed and had adequate financial resources to allow new initiatives.

The board was so impressed with Fitch's experience and expertise that his biggest problem was convincing them that he was willing to take the job. Board members asked him why he would consider leaving what appeared to be an ideal, mid-size, suburban district to come to Finley. Fitch responded that he was open to examining the opportunity further at the next step, and would look favorably on a reasonable offer from the board. The board met in a private session following Fitch's interview and concluded without much deliberation that the other two front-runners were a distant second and third to Fitch. All seven board members voted to commission the board president to extend Fitch an offer and have the board attorney negotiate a contract.

As part of the contract negotiations, Fitch asked that he be allowed to meet with the board prior to accepting the position. The request was granted and Fitch traveled to Finley.

Fitch really had three motives for calling the meeting. First, he wanted the board to know that he had the fortitude to ask quality questions of them. Second, he wanted board members to hear all of the answers in a formal setting. Finally, he wanted to get a feel for how each board member felt about relationship issues that were important to him. At the meeting, Fitch told the board that during the interview he had not had the chance to obtain some pertinent information. He asked their indulgence as he brought up specific matters that he considered significant. Initially, Fitch revealed that he had learned about individual board members by talking with constituents and gathering perceptions. Then he requested that each board member provide their opinion on the proper conduct for a school board member. That query was followed by asking how each member envisioned an ideal board-superintendent relationship. Fitch was elated that board members responded positively to his questions.

Fitch accepted the Finley superintendency mainly because of the board's commitment to improving the school district without micromanaging. He believed that Finley was a district where he could preside as a superintendent free of a school board that meddled in administrative affairs. After arriving on the job, he arranged for a retreat with the board to listen to their thoughts on the school district and establish a working relationship with them prior to their first public appearance. Out of the eight-hour planning session came seven goals for the school system, which would be translated into a working document complete with strategies and timetables for implementation. The board pledged its support for the vision that Fitch outlined, and he requested that they assemble again in 90 days to check on his progress.

Fitch spent two weeks after the retreat collecting further information about the district and assessing its strengths and weaknesses. Board members, community leaders, parents, teachers, and most administrators identified two major problems with the Finley school district: public relations and personnel concerns. Fitch's immediate course of action was to go on the stump for the school district. He launched a blitz that ultimately resulted in close to 200 public appearances—holding meetings with parents, and civic and religious groups, and taking part in interviews on radio and television. Springing new programs on an unsuspecting public had gotten the district in trouble before, and Fitch was not about to risk a repeat performance. Furthermore, involving the community in planning was one of the goals developed at the retreat with the school board. So Fitch put in place a process to ensure a wide range of stakeholders would get in on the strategy sessions.

He forged links with the community through the formation of a Public Schools Foundation and a grass roots task force for long-range planning. The task force of 40 people included local businesses, community agencies, developers, bankers, reporters, clergy, government officials, real estate agents, parents, students, and school system employees. A survey was also mailed to hundreds of Finley citizens to gather their views. In addition to task force meetings held every other month during the school year, three public hearings were scheduled to discuss district problems and listen to proposed solutions. Prior to each citizens meeting, Fitch would call in the local media and review the agenda. The public hearings were also well publicized and touted in the press to drum up attendance.

Media communication became the hallmark of the new superintendent. To encourage the healing process in the school district, Fitch met with top executives from the Finley media outlets—two daily newspapers, one weekly newspaper, and two radio stations. He asked that they get together regularly and pledged continued communication and cooperation on the part of the school district, with no surprises from his administration. Fitch also promised that he would always make himself available to the media and would never withhold information. Thus, media relations, and by extension community relations, soon became the superintendent's stock in trade.

Another issue in need of healing was the employee-management divide. As an experienced negotiator, Fitch knew the value of changing the tone of the collective bargaining process. And he was aware that the best time to approach the subject of negotiations was before an official declaration was made indicating they were needed. Fitch soon learned that a complaint or formal grievance was the standard for beginning talks with unions in the past. To shift that perspective, he began monthly meetings with union leaders to address problems before they reached the grievance stage. Fitch also appointed an assistant superintendent as the chief union negotiator to replace the board's attorney. Although the attorney was a skilled arbitrator, he lacked a professional education background and the teachers soundly rejected him. The administrator Fitch selected to handle the negotiations was a veteran educator, respected and trusted by administrators and teachers alike. Positive results were immediately realized. The teachers saw the change as a sign of good faith, and the two sides agreed to begin talks with a new spirit of cooperation and collaboration. Once the stage was set, Fitch vowed to give the negotiator full authority to reach agreements within the parameters set by the board. The last thing Fitch needed was for the teachers to believe that the negotiator was only a front and did not have the authority to make decisions.

A major task facing Fitch was transforming the school district into an organization that appreciated and practiced collaborative decision-making. Several different strategies were needed. One approach was to get the administrative staff on the same page intellectually. With his three assistant superintendents as supporters, Fitch started a reading group of central office administrators. Over several months, the administrators read about the most current best practices related to administration and collaboration. After discussing various books, the central administrators were encouraged enough to start spinoff reading groups with building level administrators and their staffs. Finally, reading groups, for teachers and members of the community, were formed. Another strategy supporting collaboration entailed helping building principals launch school improvement plans and shared decision making teams, with the central office providing the necessary autonomy to encourage such site-based actions.

Fitch modeled his expectations, with district and building level administrators as well as with teachers. He also established an annual reciprocal evaluation process because he believed that subordinates should have the opportunity to critique their supervisors. He began by asking personnel at every level to anonymously evaluate his performance. Then, to demonstrate his personal confidence in the process, Fitch made public the results of his own evaluation by subordinates and various groups. He encouraged, but did not require, all administrative staff to do the same.

The various strategies—educating people, supporting and modeling collaboration, and openly soliciting opinions of subordinates—underscored the seriousness of the cultural change for the Finley school district. As new initiatives and strategies for Finley's schools were initiated, Fitch worked with the media to keep them informed about the events happening within the district. The media, in turn, reported to the general public on what was happening under the new leadership. Change did occur in Finley. And while it was clear that change took place because of courageous and visionary leadership, the media made the change real to the public through consistent and accurate reporting. Some said that Fitch was a master at using the media to achieve his goals. However, when the question was posed to the media, they all responded that they would rather have a superintendent like Lamont Fitch—always open and communicative—than one who sought to use the media on a selective basis. In a word, the media loved Fitch and dubbed him a "mediawise superintendent."

The Finley school district was fortunate to attract Lamont Fitch, who had been highly successful in his previous superintendency. It was important to the members of the Finley school board to show the community they were seeking the best available, currently practicing superintendent for the district, based on their sense that a novice would not be acceptable. The fact that Fitch was being recruited by several school districts at the time that he was contacted by Finley only enhanced his stature as a solid choice.

His reputation for possessing unusual skills in working with the media was also proven as he went about his work. Never before had the Finley district seen a superintendent who maintained such a high profile with the entire community, let alone the media. Although the district's experience with the media had been primarily negative, and that is how most observers perceived coverage, under the leadership of Lamont Fitch the book on media relationships was rewritten. He had the ability to improve the system, and use the media to his advantage. As Finley's superintendent of schools, Fitch's leadership made a positive difference in the district for years to come.

17

Gambia: Urban Reform

School District:	Gambia—a major, urban school district with nearly 200 schools
Socioeconomics:	Mostly middle income and working poor
Demographics:	140,000 students; a diverse mix with 35 percent Hispanic, 39 percent African American, and 6 percent Asian or other
Superintendent:	Montell Gable—an experienced superintendent from another state

Boasting of having the largest number of Fortune 500 companies outside of New York city, Gambia is home to business and industry that provides the economic base for a metropolitan area of nearly three million people. While well-structured highways keep traffic moving past upscale business parks and major hotel chains by day, driving into the metropolis at night it is truly a sight to behold, as the lights that illuminate the glitz and glitter of the downtown buildings can be seen for miles. The approach to the city includes suburban communities that merge into one another and cross the city borders without losing their own identity; the causal visitor would not be able to discern where one municipality begins and another ends. The suburbs surrounding Gambia include many spacious and affluent homes, along with modest but well-tended middle income settlements. The city neighborhoods hold a mixture of larger, older homes and smaller, more closely spaced, traditional, urban housing. Apartments abound in both the city and suburbs. The suburban apartments tend to be upscale, with higher rent, while the city offers bargains due to the advanced age of some of its complexes. Like many urban settings, some areas of the city are far more expensive to live in than any of the surrounding suburbs. The same is true for some of the more traditional, upscale, downtown hotels.

The parts of Gambia that most visitors don't see are the distressed neighborhoods and public housing projects. Although some of the older homes were originally well-built and designed for middle-to upper-income citizens, they now house low-income residents and have become a haven for the working poor and recent immigrants. And the public housing projects tend to provide a home for residents who rely on government subsidies, or are exclusively supported by welfare. Recognizing the negative impact of so many poor people living in concentrated areas, the city developed a program to eliminate some of the public housing apartments and replace them with single-family homes. Urban renewal, coupled with restructuring dwellings for the city's impoverished, has been a priority for Gambia. With city leaders concerned that Gambia has more than its share of poor, homeless, and disenfranchised people, this proud city is continually working to improve its image.

The Gambia school district serves 140,000 students in nearly 200 schools. This major, urban school system primarily educates students who reside within the city of Gambia, but it is also home to students who live in three adjacent, smaller municipalities. Gambia's school system could be considered an anomaly among urban school districts. Like many large, urban systems, Gambia continues to experience increases in enrollment due to the influx of immigrants. While many school systems similarly situated have realized declining economic resources in the face of a growing population, that's not been the case with Gambia. Even with the albatross of two-decades-old, court ordered desegregation, the economic resources of Gambia's public schools have managed to remain stable.

Following desegregation, white and middle-class flight has been a constant. The goal of many young families is to save enough money to buy a house in the suburbs by the time their children reach school age. Thus, the city's demographics bear no resemblance to the school system's student population. The breakdown of Gambia's population of one million is 48 percent white, 25 percent Hispanic, 22 percent African American, and 5 percent Asian or other. In the school district, however, 35 percent of the students are Hispanic, 39 percent are African American, 20 percent are white, and 6 percent are Asian or other. More than 75 percent of the district's students qualify for the free lunch program.

The city is dominated by an elite, white power structure that has enormous influence over school matters. Far from giving up on Gambia's schools, city leaders have historically embraced the school district as being important to the vitality of the city and the region. The power players who actually own and run the city make conscious decisions to support the schools. They take great interest in the district, sponsoring school board members and ensuring that city leaders always know where the system stands economically. Whenever the school system needs funds to increase services or build additional structures, the behind-the-scenes power brokers decide whether or not it is necessary. If they think the need is genuine, they support it, even if it means a public vote. And Gambia's residents tend to back school propositions for more funding when the power brokers give the signal to do so.

The "power," and to a large extent the control of the district, remains with the city's elite partly because of the makeup of the school board. Although the Gambia school district serves an 80 percent minority student population, five of its nine board members are white, three are black, and one is Hispanic. Some may claim that race does not make a difference, but this board—basically professional people who are respected by their communities—is clearly divided philosophically along racial lines. The black board members support and promote issues that are important to blacks, while the lone Hispanic board member generally sides with the white board members.

When Gambia's superintendent of eight years announced that he would be retiring after one more year, the school board started thinking about his replacement. In spite of its challenges, the Gambia school system had enjoyed stable leadership. The impending departure would mark the beginning of the board's search for only the fourth district superintendent in 48 years. To start the process, the board decided not to employ a traditional search firm. Instead, they agreed to identify a panel of six experts from around the country who were considered leaders in the business of identifying outstanding superintendents. Some members of the panel were from universities, while others were highly regarded former or practicing superintendents. The panel was instructed by the school board to recruit the best candidates nationwide who had the background and characteristics to successfully lead the Gambia school district. The board left it up to the panel as to how they would attract candidates, however they did provide some general guidelines. First, they insisted that the candidates have a solid track record of success. Second, they suggested that the candidates have experience working in large, urban school districts with diverse student populations. Third, they stated that they desired candidates from districts with 50,000 students or more, which they later modified to 25,000 at the urging of the panel. The board made no reference to racial preference, yet when queried by the panel, they said they were interested in the best candidates, regardless of race or gender. The panel began its work by meeting and brainstorming about candidates who would have the credentials to fit the criteria established by the Gambia school board. Together they identified potential applicants and ended up with a list of 30 people to whom they sent letters of invitation. The letters were sent out in May even though the vacancy was 14 months away. The position was also advertised in the usual trade journals, and at colleges and universities across the country.

Dr. Montell Gable, a 43-year-old black male, was in his second year as superintendent of a much-acclaimed school district when he received his invitation letter from the panel. The letter and the unique approach used to identify superintendent candidates for one of the nation's largest school systems intrigued him. Looking over the list of those on the panel, Gable recognized the names of some of the most respected school leaders in the business. While he was impressed, he laid the letter aside and went about his duties. Several weeks went by and Gable kept the letter on top of his desk with the intention of discarding it later. Although he had heard of Gambia, he could not bring himself to look beyond the position he occupied so early in his tenure.

In July, as fate would have it, Gable was attending a church revival in the community where he was superintendent and learned that the evangelist who was preaching was a pastor in the city of Gambia. Throughout the program that evening, Gable could not stop thinking about the coincidence of the Gambia connection. Following the meeting, he went up to the minister, introduced himself as the local school superintendent, and asked if the minister would be willing to have lunch with him the following day. Without further explanation from Gable, the minister consented. At lunch the following day, Gable and the minister got along so well that is was hard to believe they were strangers. Gable told the minister that he had received an invitation to apply for the superintendent of schools position at Gambia and wanted to know if the minister could fill him in on the school district and the community. The minister shared what little he knew about the Gambia school district and departed with a promise that he would call Gable in a few days with more thorough information.

On the next day, Gable telephoned one of the panel members who had signed the letter of invitation that he had received. The conversation was positive, with the panelist affirming support for Gable's application. The panelist did express, however, that Gable was superintendent of the smallest district among the 30 superintendents who were invited to apply. At 15,000 students, Gable's district was even smaller than the threshold that the panel had established with the board. But the entire panel had agreed that Gable's record of success and stature as a superintendent made him a good competitor, and in his case the requirement was overlooked. The panel member further stated that screening for the first round of interviews would take place the following week, and Gable needed to submit his application within seven days to be considered. Their goal was to review credentials and reduce the field of applicants to 12 before the first round of interviews were to begin. Meanwhile, Gable received the follow-up phone call from the minister, who encouraged him to apply, based on positive feedback he received when investigating the Gambia school district.

After consulting with his family, the school board president, and the local newspaper editor—all of whom agreed to hold the information in confidence—Gable submitted his application for the superintendent's position in the Gambia school district. Ten days later he received a call from one of the panelists informing him that he was one of 12 semifinalists. The next step would be an interview with the panel so that they could narrow the field to five and present them to the school board. Gable's interview with the panel went very well, yet they reminded him that he was considered a longshot due to the size of his school district. The panel deliberated and made their decision. A week later a panelist contacted Gable and informed him that he had made the cut as one of five finalists and would be interviewed by the Gambia school board.

Given the short tenure in his superintendency, and the very positive relationship he had established with the board, staff, and community, Gable felt compelled once again to visit the local newspaper editor in his own district. This time the editor said he could no longer keep the information confidential due to the status of Gable's candidacy. He did agree, however, to make sure that Gable's involvement with the Gambia search was presented in the best possible light so as not to damage his credibility with the local community. The board president in Gable's district was disappointed that Gable was pursing another superintendency, but he agreed to support Gable in discussing the matter with the full board in a closed session. In the meeting, Gable explained that his application was a professional obligation due the nature of the invitation and the stature of the Gambia school district. He said he felt it was a credit to his district that he would even be considered for the position and thought of so highly. He added that his candidacy was a long shot, and he did not expect to be offered the job. Gable met with his administrative staff and key community constituents to alert them in advance of the public announcement regarding his candidacy that was to come via the local newspaper. Three days before Gable's interview, the newspaper ran the story with the following headline: Gambia School District Courts Montell Gable. The body of the story reflected the same tone. Gable not only had avoided a potential public relations disaster in his school district, he had in fact successfully created a positive story.

Gable arrived in Gambia two days prior to his scheduled interview with the school board. He had already studied media accounts of the various issues in the school district and was basically familiar with the challenges facing a new superintendent. He also had read media reports on the other four candidates after their interviews with the Gambia school board. The competitors presented a strong challenge and Gable knew them all by reputation. The Gambia media actively followed the story of the candidates for a superintendent, and based on information from school board members, tentatively ranked them leading up to Gable's interview.

Gables felt positive chemistry between himself and the Gambia board members during his interview. The fact that it lasted for an hour beyond the scheduled time was a signal that the interview had gone well. Throughout the meeting Gable was assertive and answered all of the questions posed to him clearly and succinctly. He strategically mentioned that he had spent two days in Gambia prior to his interview. He even commented on a student athletic event that he had attended at a Gambia high school. When Gable saw openings to interject, he made it known to the board that he had the skills needed to achieve the goals sought by the district. To further illustrate his point, Gable methodically walked board members through a process that he would use to engage the various constituents in school district matters. The board was obviously impressed.

Following Gable's interview, media leaks revealed that he and another candidate were the front-runners for Gambia's school superintendent. Yet the board decided to visit the home districts of all five finalists rather than prematurely dismiss any of them. It was Gable's understanding all along that the board was working well in advance of the incumbent's retirement; the incumbent was to leave the position on June 30 and the school year was just getting underway. The site visits by the Gambia board to the candidates' home turf were scheduled in the same order as the interviews. In an unusual display of interest, all nine Gambia board members participated in the site visits.

By the time the board members made their trip to Gable's district, it was October. Their visit to Gable's district not only went smoothly, they spent two full days meeting with every sector of the community to learn more about Gable. Just prior to their departure, the board members asked Gable to meet with them at their hotel. At the meeting, they admitted to Gable that they had conferred and were unanimous in their resolve to offer him the Gambia superintendency. Their original time line had to be modified, they informed him, due to the incumbent announcing he would be leaving on January 30, rather than June 30, to accept another position. The board asked Gable to begin his new duties in Gambia on February 1. Gable was startled, but direct: He could not accept the job. He had a commitment to work until the end of the school year and he would not betray his employer's trust.

The Gambia school board was not expecting a rejection, but they told Gable they respected his decision and they returned to Gambia. Gable met with his board in a closed session the very next day and relayed the events as they had occurred. He also restated his pledge to not abandon the school district at midyear. The school board accepted his decision as a matter of personal integrity and supported his desire not to discuss it further. Having returned home, the Gambia school board debated the need to decide on a second choice for school superintendent. After hours of discussion, the board could not agree. Hopelessly deadlocked, they finally decided to telephone Gable and suggest a compromise. The board proposed that Gable secure permission from his own board to spend one week per month in Gambia—from February 1 until June 30—while maintaining his position in his home district. The plan included an interim superintendent in Gambia during the three weeks that Gable was away. Upon hearing the proposal, Gable agreed to test the idea with his board president.

Gable's board president was supportive and assisted him in discussing the proposal with the rest of the board in a closed session. Accepting the alternative arrangement, Gable hammered out a contract with the Gambia school district. He selected the second week of the month to spend in Gambia so that he would not miss any board meetings in his own district. Also, the second week was an opportunity to interact with the Gambia school board in one of its two regular monthly meetings. For five months Gable worked in both districts. The size of the Gambia district required a great deal of time just to become familiar with the basics. The consultive period turned out to be a good experience, allowing Gable to listen and learn without the pressure of the full superintendency. Gambia's board was patient and allowed Gable to set his own schedule during the interim period. During those five months of commuting to Gambia, Gable described his most immediate challenges as: 1.) improving student achievement; 2.) shifting the staff's focus from business issues to the education program; 3.) establishing a reasonable timeline to gain permission from the federal court to release the school district from court ordered desegregation; 4.) reorganizing the administrative staff; 5.) boosting the morale of employees in the system; and 6.) working with the board and community to develop a comprehensive strategic plan to guide the district over the next five years. Gable used his observations to create a document, and prepared to meet with the Gambia school board in his first retreat with them after July 1, when his full-time contract with Gambia would begin.

Gable's first retreat with the Gambia school board was held the second week of July. Both he and the board were glad that his awkward months of commuting had come to an end. Gable's goal for the retreat was to come away with a full understanding of his future working relationship with the board. He also wanted to elicit their ideas about the immediate challenges facing the district prior to presenting his own observations. While Gable achieved all of the goals he had for the retreat, he found that the political, philosophical, and racial division among board members ran deeper than it appeared. The divide was especially apparent with the three black board members, who were isolated and patronized. Although they knew they were outnumbered, they never backed down from asserting their beliefs.

Their mistreatment was obvious, prompting reactions of defensiveness and hostility from them. Gable saw that the five white board members, supported by their Hispanic colleague, would give the impression that they were listening and considering the viewpoints of the black board members, but the majority would use their power to control board actions.

Despite the fact that political and racial issues had often overshadowed educational issues, all board members were sensitive to the city of Gambia's public image and wanted the school district be viewed in a positive light. Throughout the first year and beyond, the board members were very supportive of Gable as a leader. Yet because of the size and complexity of the school district, issues seemed to require long deliberations to reach any resolution. Meetings often took on the flavor of a debate rather than a discussion among the board members. While this was somewhat frustrating to Gable, he recognized the posturing and positioning and did not take their political maneuvers personally. What was difficult to accept was the constant reference to race. The scars left by desegregation were deep. The school district was still under a federal court order to desegregate, which was a sore point with most citizens. The white board members unanimously felt that the court order needed to be lifted from the district; the black board members were suspicious of their motives. The lone Hispanic board member tended to be neutral, yet would opt for release from the court when pressed for an opinion.

As an administrator who was committed to providing the best education possible for all students, Gable's position was to move forward and persevere in spite of the court order. He made it clear to the board and the community that his goal as the superintendent of Gambia's schools was to relieve the district from the federal court order as quickly as possible. This position did not sit well with the black board members, who openly told Gable that he was on the wrong side of the issue. Gable, however, held firm to his belief and nevertheless continued to be an assertive leader. Over time, the black board members accepted Gable's resolve, but continued to fight behind the scenes to ensure the court order remained in place until such time that the district could prove all vestiges of discrimination had been removed from the school system. The black board members regularly gave examples as to why the school district was not ready to have the court order rescinded. During such pronouncements, the white board members would counter with their reasons as to why it should be, often citing the support of the superintendent and a majority of the community. It seemed to be a situation without a solution. Yet the black board members appeared to have the attention of the federal judge who was assigned to oversee the case; the judge was reluctant to remove the court order until the black board members were satisfied with the progress of the Gambia district.

In spite of the great racial divide in the school district, Gable managed to enjoy the support of the entire school board and the Gambia community for his expertise and professionalism. His popularity extended across racial lines to the city fathers, the business community, the parent-teacher associations, and internal constituents, which included teachers and other employees. Gable was considered by all to be a leader who was a good listener and attentive to concerns. His plans for reforming the school system were hardly debated by the school board, and generally accepted and implemented with enthusiasm by the staff and everyone else involved.

Gable's accomplishments during his tenure with Gambia schools included creating a leaner organization, saving taxpayers $6 million in the process. He recultured the school district from a top-down management system to a unique form of site-based management that he called *School Centered Education*. He explained the plan as one in which a school system becomes a "system of schools," and under the new management format, principals and faculty members are held accountable for improved student achievement. Gable implemented a $3 million School Performance Incentive Awards program to reward top performing schools and staffs for improvements in student test scores. He marshaled support for and was successful in getting voters to approve a $300 million bond program so several new schools could be built and others could be upgraded.

Gable also came up with a novel way to study reforms and implement them in the school district by selecting creative leaders in the system to conduct research and study groups that would examine unique approaches to urban school reform. In all, Gable had 16 study groups working simultaneously, and dubbed the effort Options for the Nineties. Some of the options that were studied, and ultimately put into practice, were: a pilot of year-round schools; an electronic school; and a new course requirement in citizenship and character development.

Student test scores not only improved under Gable's leadership, they were the best in a decade. Students placed above the state averages in all categories and the dropout rate was reduced from 21 percent to 6 percent. Teacher training was revamped to be results-oriented and teacher-driven, rather than administrator-driven, and tied to a new accountability effort. Volunteers donated over 700,000 hours per year to Gambia's schools during Gable's tenure. The district gained a new library automation system, new computers in all of its schools, a multicultural/multiethnic plan, and a reading initiative that made all teachers "teachers of reading." In addition, Gable led state capital efforts to resolve statewide issues in school finance. Thus, the school board, while racially and philosophically divided, generally agreed that superintendent Montell Gable was the type of leader the Gambia school district needed, and they were glad they were able to retain such a skilled professional.

A high profile district and one of the largest in the country, Gambia presented many challenges to its new superintendent, Dr. Montell Gable, not the least of which was a racially divided community and school board. The essential task for a superintendent in Gambia was to stay focused on the main mission—educating students—in the midst of constant political infighting and racial animosity. All of this was occurring while some segments of the community and some school board members worked feverishly to resist the quest by district leaders to be released from court ordered desegregation. Gable demonstrated that a good superintendent could walk the tightrope and remain victorious. To be successful in his position in Gambia, as Gable was, took an enormous amount of courage and determination to press forward with a positive education agenda in spite of serious obstacles that were always present, and that had nothing to do with education.

18

Harrow: A Turnaround Challenge

School District:	Harrow—kindergarten through grade 12
Socioeconomics:	Surburban, with urban or rural areas; wealthy, to very economically diverse
Demographics:	30,000 students; 35 percent minority
Superintendent:	Jermaine Hardy—formerly a superintendent in a large, urban district out of state

Harrow is a school community about 40 miles from a major, midwestern city and by definition is suburban, although it holds pockets that are urban or rural. The Harrow district serves 30,000 students, of which 65 percent are white, 22 percent and growing are Hispanic, 8 percent are African American, and 5 percent are Asian. While larger than most of the neighboring school districts, Harrow is not unlike the suburban districts that make up the ring surrounding most major cities. But it does present a unique challenge. The district includes 10 separate municipalities within its borders, with towns that range from very wealthy to very economically diverse. None of them are considered poor, but at least three contain distressed areas, and they seem to bring the greatest concern to the school system. Most of the students from those areas are also minority, and often require special interventions to keep pace with educational expectations. The mix of poverty and race has brought resentment from residents of the wealthier and primarily white areas of the district, to the extent that movements to leave the Harrow district, or disconnect from it, occur from time to time. On the other hand, district officials tout Harrow's racial and social diversity as a strength, and spend time and resources on maintaining harmony among the many communities.

Also different from most districts, Harrow has experienced exponential growth. The district has grown so much that keeping up financially has been a major battle. Despite Harrow's best efforts to cut expenditures over the years in order to balance its budget, the district has continued to fight an enormous deficit in its operating funds. Of course Harrow's citizens have become increasingly critical of the school district due to its instability and struggles to afford basic necessities. And the toll taken on the school district has gone so far as to damage its reputation.

In addition to the cashflow shortage for normal operations, the Harrow district's staff—particularly the teachers—have added to the financial pressure. Dissatisfied with wages, they have frequently argued for a pay increase, and have even gone on strike in an attempt to achieve their goal. The strikes have been very bitter, dividing the school community and turning many constituents against the district. Some citizens have blamed the teachers for the dispute, while others have faulted the school board or the administration. Nevertheless, the shortage of money and the resulting teacher strikes put such a strain on the school district that it lost the support of both its internal and external publics.

Ironically, regardless of its history of financial challenges and employee upheaval, the Harrow district has managed to maintain stable leadership. This 150-year-old district has had only three superintendents serve in the past 40 years. District critics have suggested that prior boards continued to support past superintendents beyond the time they were effective, assuming that new leadership on a more regular basis might have kept the district from becoming complacent. It was a gradual turnover of the school board that prompted a search for a new superintendent in Harrow. The superintendent in office at the time saw the handwriting on the wall and sought release from his contract, thus freeing the board to advertise for a new district leader.

The search firm the Harrow district commissioned to attract potential superintendent candidates recruited Jermaine Hardy. In its recruitment effort, the search firm leveled with Hardy about the challenges related to the district and the never-ending problem of financial shortfalls. While cautious in contemplating leaving the secure situation where he was superintendent, Hardy was curious about the opportunity in Harrow. After continual coaxing by the search firm, and personal investigation, Hardy agreed to apply for the Harrow superintendency. Among the applicants who were recruited for the position, Hardy was the practicing superintendent with the highest profile. Moreover, his record of success as a superintendent was known throughout the nation. Once Harrow school board members discovered that Hardy was considering the district's superintendency, they seemed to be united in their desire to maintain his interest in the position. District observers quickly concluded that although the board had identified and interviewed four finalists, the entire board could agree on only one—Jermaine Hardy. Following the traditional two interviews, the Harrow school board concurred that Hardy was the finalist on which to concentrate, and scheduled a site visit to his home district. After three days of interviewing various constituents, the board was more convinced than ever that they had found their new superintendent. All that was left was for Hardy to formally accept, and for the two parties to negotiate provisions of a contract. To the board's delight, an agreement was reached. Hardy became the fourth superintendent appointed in the Harrow school district in 40 years.

Hardy began his tenure with his new district by making trips to Harrow during the four months preceding his official start date. His home district permitted him to use accumulated vacation days to travel to Harrow to begin his personal orientation. Prior to accepting the position, Hardy had studied the various issues plaguing the school district, but he was anxious to learn more from the district's stakeholders. During his visits to Harrow, Hardy set up meetings with every conceivable group that was active within the school community to get to know Harrow's internal and external publics. But the answer to being able to overcome the obstacles in Harrow, Hardy felt, was finding out more about the controversies within the district. A major player—and often a source of public discontent—was the teachers' union. Hardy spent hours listening to union leaders to understand the district from their point of view. He did the same with the other unions in the school district, often hosting breakfast or luncheon meetings at sites away from the district offices. Hardy also took the time to hear the concerns of parents and community groups, and extended himself to the business community, as he made his way across the district in his listening sessions.

Finally, one group to which Hardy paid special attention was the Harrow media. Up to, and including the time of Hardy's appointment, many thought of the news media as an enemy of the school district, especially the district's employees. Even the Harrow school board had become suspicious of the media's motives, with regard to what the board believed was a less than balanced approach taken when it came to school district news. A major newspaper article preceding Hardy's arrival to the Harrow district featured a photo of him, along with the headline "Joining the Struggle." The accompanying story was typical of the negative slant Harrow's media put on school district reports.

After his four months of visits and listening sessions in Harrow, Hardy officially began his contractual duties on July 1. His first goal was to set a time for the school board to meet with him prior to the first, public school board meeting. The board agreed, and the date was set for a two-day board-superintendent retreat within a week of his arrival in the district. During the retreat, the Board allowed Hardy to take the lead. He was fully prepared with written material, along with charts and graphs. In his presentation, Hardy highlighted his findings from all of the listening sessions he conducted throughout the district. He used a format that initially allowed the board to view the problems he found, as enumerated by the various constituent groups, and followed the problem identification process with possible solutions. The board occasionally interjected with comments, but basically spent the entire first day listening to Hardy's observations.

By the second day, Hardy was fully engaging the board in individual and group problem identification. After a number of observations by the board, members began to merge their thoughts and categorize issues into common themes. Ultimately, the board and Hardy agreed on seven major issues that required immediate attention in the school district. While there were many more, the board and superintendent felt that these had to be tackled as the top priority:

- A massive public relations overhaul
- Improving finances, including increasing revenue
- Boosting student achievement
- Addressing staff morale and labor issues
- Monitoring, containing, and adequately funding growth
- Improving media relationships
- Developing a long-range strategic plan for improving the district

The superintendent and board planned a series of retreats for the purpose of charting progress from year to year on the various goals. They agreed to three retreats per year for the dual purpose of evaluating the performance of the superintendent and board, and modifying and adding goals as needed on an annual basis.

Following the first year of Hardy's tenure, and him working closely with the community, it was no coincidence that a long-range, strategic plan with 168 recommendations for improving the district was adopted. After successfully completing the goals, the plan was updated with 140 action strategies for increasing the quality of education over a five-year period. A report about the school district after the fifth year, written and published by a local university, stated that Harrow had accomplished much since the district asked voters to approve a referendum. In fact, just four years before, voters had been asked to approve two ballot issues: authorizing the sale of bonds for facility improvements, and authorizing an increase in the tax rate for education programs and operating costs. The success of both referendums played a pivotal role in allowing Harrow to make tremendous progress. Thanks to the community's generosity, the district was able to reverse a downward financial spiral, eliminating millions of dollars of accumulated budget deficit and building a reserve that served as a cushion for possible future financial shortfalls. In related efforts, management, employees, and the community joined together to develop a collaborative, decision making model that allowed the various stakeholders to have a say in how decisions affecting the school district were made. Most importantly, the additional resources made it possible to broaden opportunities for students and staff, resulting in steady improvements in classroom achievement.

The following are some of the benefits realized since Hardy became superintendent:

- Curriculum in every major instructional area was reviewed and revised, with particular emphasis on reading, mathematics, and science. New textbooks were added and library collections rebuilt.

- The district became a technology leader, with each school wired and tied to the Internet. Thousands of computers were placed in classrooms and labs, and were key to the learning program. Library collections were enhanced through online connections, and video monitors tied classrooms together throughout the district.

- Placing major emphasis on helping the youngest students get a strong start in school, the district's programs for preschool children were expanded, kindergarten opportunities were added, and teachers developed a new kindergarten curriculum. The average class size was also lowered throughout the district.

- Labor strife became a thing of the past after a new method was put in place for discussing issues with all employee groups before they became problems.

- Additional resources were invested in reading programs in schools with high concentrations of at-risk students, defined as students in danger of not being promoted at the elementary and middle schools levels.

- Academy programs designed to give students a head start on their higher education, and unique to the area surrounding the school district as well as much of the state, were added at each of the four high schools: science and engineering at one school; gifted and talented at another; visual and performing arts at the third; and world languages and international studies at the fourth.

- Career and technical education programs were revamped to offer cutting-edge opportunities for high school students interested in gaining marketable skills.

- Composite results on the ACT college entrance exams were higher than they had ever been at each high school, or in each subject area tested. Most importantly, they were above state and national averages.

- The school district produced a record 28 National Merit Scholars and 50 National Merit Commended Students who ranked in the top 5 percent of the merit competition. At the same time, more than 100 students were named National Advanced Placement Scholars as a result of high scores on college level tests.

- District students consistently maintained math scores above state averages on the state's testing program. On the most recent reading exam given by the state, the Harrow district's students scored higher at every grade level.

- Results were at or above national norms in every subject area tested on the Iowa Tests of Basic Skills, the standardized test used by the district.

Yes, the Harrow school district was quite a different place under Jermaine Hardy's leadership, who took on a school district with a severely damaged reputation. The general consensus between school board members and within the community was that Harrow had waited too long to address the need for a serious overhaul. However the board was adamant that it would take a proven and respected leader to champion the district and change its course, or it was not going to happen. Harrow got all that it bargained for when Hardy was selected superintendent. The school board believed that securing his services represented a good return on the voters' investment, being that he was recruited based on his record of success as a superintendent in other school districts across the country.

The shift in the Harrow school district was noticeable almost immediately once Hardy took over. Not only the board, but the community was thankful for someone who was able to lead the effort in turning the district around. Hardy's skill in working with internal and external stakeholders won him favor, which shows how a district can respond if there is enough confidence in its leader. The record of accomplishments by Hardy and the district in just a few years was impressive, and demonstrates that with the proper foresight and leadership by a superintendent, almost anything is possible. But even Hardy was quick to point out that positive change does not occur unless significant constituents in the school district and community agree on what needs to be done and work together.

Part IV
CONCLUSION

The Superintendent of the Future

Many progressive superintendents across the country already comprehend and practice "good leadership." But to be successful in the 21st century, superintendents must adapt to the continually emerging role of the superintendency. Throughout the chapters of this book, the enlightened superintendent of the 21st century was held up as the model for the way in which contemporary leadership should be undertaken. Unfortunately, not all sectors of society have yet grasped the meaning of what makes a superintendent a successful leader in today's world. In many school systems, for example, superintendents are portrayed as managers. School boards and communities in such systems generally demand sound fiscal management, and expect the school system to run like a business. They want educational accountability and strong achievement numbers, but the bottom line on the balance sheet is what seems to get the real attention. When topics such as fiscal integrity, efficiency, and personnel management captivate a large share of the headlines, it seems contrary to what is most often stated as the main mission of an education system. There are stories over the past 20 years or so where superintendents were extremely popular, and in every sense competent in their work, but they lost favor upon their departure when the financial condition of the school district was found to be different than reported. Those situations are unfortunate, especially when the departing superintendent may be seeking a new position in another district and has to deal with explaining how the financial conditions took such a negative turn.

The larger the district, the less likely it is that the superintendent will have the time to personally monitor the accuracy of financial reports. The same is true of the school board. As individuals or a body, the school board cannot really verify the correctness of the figures. They, as well as the superintendent, must rely on the competence, honesty, and integrity of the people who are charged with keeping them informed about the district's true fiscal condition. In addition, the school board is required to employ an independent auditing service as a neutral third party to inspect the books on an annual basis. Unfortunately, stories abound about the failure of a school system's internal business staff due to incompetence or dishonesty. Obviously, if a school district has a business staff that is inept or deceptive, coupled with an internal auditing process that does not detect financial problems, there is always the possibility of a crisis. Exactly how is a superintendent supposed to prevent this from happening? As stated earlier, no matter how well the responsibilities of the superintendency are handled, the blame for financial mismanagement will land squarely upon the superintendent. All that will matter in the end is that both the school board and the superintendent failed in their fiduciary duty to local taxpayers. And depending upon the seriousness of the budget crisis, it could cost the superintendent his or her job (Wallace, 2005).

In addition to the preoccupation with the business aspect of school leadership, there is the assumption of political acumen. To be successful, the superintendent has to know who the district's constituents are and what they want. The constituent base differs from one superintendency to another, depending on the makeup of the school system. Communities across the country have become increasingly diverse over the years, which has intensified both conflict and politics in public education (Kowalski, 1999). Diversity, in this context, spans more than race and ethnicity. It also includes those needing special education, the physically handicapped, the gifted, and the homeless, to name a few. And the list seems to grow with each passing decade. As a result, demands for resources are coming from more special interest groups than ever before, and the public's demand for participation in school affairs is extremely vocal. Add to that mix the strengthened role of the federal government and state departments of education, armed with their legislative mandates for improvement that are often without accompanying funding. Although politics and bureaucracy may be prime irritants to district leaders, concerns about financing, especially when it comes to unfunded mandates, are causing additional pressure. In a survey by Public Agenda, almost 9 out of 10 superintendents stated that federal mandates are increasing, but resources needed to fulfill them are not forthcoming (Public Agenda Online, 2001). Also, it would appear that the emphasis is more on compliance than improving education (Carter & Cunningham, 1997).

The federal government and the courts have moved to center stage with involvement in public education that is quite different from their traditional role. The result is that education now has a prime spot in the political arena (Hayes, 2001). Consider, for instance, the federal government's mandate that all schools adhere to a single standard as expressed in the 2001 reauthorization of the Elementary and Secondary Education Act of 1965—known as the No Child Left Behind (NCLB) law—which adds to the confusion of what is expected of school leaders. One provision of the law requires that states test all students in grades three through eight annually. The tests must be standards-based and allow for comparing schools and school districts within the state. The law also requires "highly qualified teachers" in every subject taught, without clearly defining who is considered highly qualified. The reporting requirements to parents and the community are enormous. Districts are ordered to prepare and distribute report cards to citizens within their boundaries, in which they must include data on student progress for the district and for each school (Hoyle, et al., 2005).

Every state, district, and school will be required to make adequate yearly progress toward reaching state standards (Harvey, 2005c). But requirements within the law are still vague. As of this point, states and districts are still debating the definition of *adequate yearly progress* and whom it includes. Under the guidelines of NCLB, students are categorized by subgroups, such as those based on race, ethnicity, disabilities, and economic condition to determine how well schools are meeting their needs (Hoyle, et al., 2005). Schools then pass or fail the yearly progress standard based on how they fare with each subgroup. All of the schools in a district will be required to show that there is no gap between the performance of students in any of the subgroups (Harvey, 2005c).

Thousands of schools will be labeled as "failing," some of which will not deserve such a label. And some schools that are providing second-rate instruction won't be considered inadequate (Popham, 2004). It has been reported that, according to the rules, if a school fails with just one subgroup, it is considered a failing school. Therefore, even if a small group of foreign children arrived in the district a little more than a year ago, their low scores would cause their school to be designated as a failing school (Popham, 2004). When the NCLB act went into effect in the 2002-2003 school year, early indications revealed that, depending upon definitions, up to 85 percent of schools that receive federal funding in some states may be unable to meet the new standards (Harvey, 2005c).

The penalties schools and districts face for failing to meet the new accountability-driven standards are significant (Harvey, 2005c). By 2014, if schools are not showing "adequate yearly progress" in closing the gap, the state may redirect district funds to pay for remedial efforts such as tutors, counseling, or private schooling (Fuller & Harvey, 2005), or it may result in state takeovers (Harvey, 2005c). Under one provision of the law, schools, not school districts, that do not make the prescribed adequate yearly progress for two consecutive years must allow students to transfer to a school of their choice that is performing better. Yet there is confusion about this transfer rule. It is not clear whether a student is restricted to transferring to a better school within his or her own district, or if it is possible for a student to transfer to a school in another district within the state, or even across state lines.

The U.S. Supreme Court limits the extent of federal involvement in education based on Constitutional provisions. And the U.S. Constitution grants legal responsibility for education to state governments (Hoyle, et al., 2005). So regardless of the intent of the law and its various interpretations, a basic question remains: When the federal role in education is not mentioned in the United States Constitution, what is the constitutionality of a federal law that prescribes, in such a detailed way, what states should do and how they should do it? As we look at what we know about the silence of the federal Constitution on the government's responsibility for education, and the historical role of the state's responsibility, there have been a number of legal challenges to the constitutionality of the federal government's involvement as it relates to this mandate.

Some communities have reacted strongly to the NCLB law, arguing that the fixation on standards is hurting too many children (Hayes, 2001). The pressure of reform mandates, and the NCLB act in particular, has actually led to situations where major cities have taken over the school systems and all but separated from the state. Not only educators, but legislators and entire states have been rebelling over the law (Wood, 2004). By early 2004, resolutions in 12 states were either pending or enacted in opposition to elements of NCLB (Harvey, 2005c). The vote was almost unanimous by legislatures in Utah and Virginia to not comply. Hawaii, Arizona, New Mexico, and Vermont rejected some or all of NCLB's provisions. And one of the strangest results of the NCLB law is that many states actually lowered their testing standards so that most of their schools would not be declared failing (Hammond-Darling, 2004).

The common expectation for a new superintendent in today's climate is to have the ability to reform the education system (Hayes, 2001), which is supported by the fact that "school reform" is the national battle cry. Somewhere along the way in the past 20 years, perhaps fueled by the 1983 Nation At Risk report, it was decided that schooling in the United States was in dire need of reform. The country, through then Secretary of Education Terrell Bell, decided that U.S. schools were not providing an adequate education for the students they served. Since that time, the federal government has been searching for a way to influence American schools and create the massive improvement they see as necessary. Many recommendations have come in the form of mandates, with the expectations that school boards, superintendents, and local school districts would respond (Carter & Cunningham, 1997). The reform movement continued in the 1990s, with most states developing assessment programs to monitor the progress of students and schools. That put considerable pressure on school boards, superintendents, principals, and teachers to boost student scores on state and national tests (Glass, 2000d). The federal government's Goal 2000 initiative and its successors were attempted, but to no real avail. Granted, some school systems across the country paid attention and worked toward providing better schooling. Some states also announced and implemented their own brands of reform, and in many cases shook the status quo. By and large, however, there remained major federal dissatisfaction with our nation's schools. But it was not until the 2001 No Child Left Behind law was enacted that all public schools in the country were thrown into the middle of mandated reform.

As schools must increasingly answer to the public, the superintendent's survival depends more heavily on the ability to improve the achievement levels of students (Hayes, 2001). And never before have district leaders been required to track student progress so closely. Besides creating ongoing stress, that pressure is also contributing to superintendent turnover (Harvey & Wallace, 2005), although there is disagreement as to just how bad the situation really is. A study in 2000 by the American Association of School Administrators (AASA) entitled *Career Crisis in the Superintendency?* found that 92 percent of the superintendents surveyed were concerned with high turnover in the profession, while 88 percent believed there is an applicant shortage and a "serious crisis" facing the superintendency (Cooper, et al., 2000). The turnover of superintendents reached a high in 1991, with a tenure of less than 5 years for superintendents nationwide, and 2.5 to 3 years for those in larger, urban school districts (Houston, 1997).

The average length of tenure for superintendents in a 10-year study by the AASA in 1992 was found to be 6.4 years. Another AASA 10-year study in 2000 reported that superintendents held their jobs for between 5 and 6 years, however the decline in tenure was attributed to the unusual number of superintendents just entering the profession at the time. Data also showed that 41.3 percent of the superintendents had been in the position for 10 or more years. For the largest urban districts, the story was different. There, 4.7 years was the mean. Yet most superintendents reported spending over half of their superintendency in only one district, 24.5 percent in two superintendencies, and 11.8 percent in three (Glass, 2000b). And *Career Crisis in the School Superintendency?* (Cooper, et al., 2000) confirmed that the superintendency may not be quite as unstable as perceptions would lead one to believe. That study found that superintendents had been in their current positions for 7.25 years. While there are many causes for superintendents to move on to another position, the main reasons cited by most are better pay and responsibility (Glass, 1992).

On the other hand, the length of time needed to fill superintendency positions has increased, with some suggesting it is because of fewer qualified applicants (Houston, 1997). Others propose that the applicant pool is simply different. For one, there are more women applying for the job (Tallerico, 2000). However, by and large school district leadership still does not mirror district demographics. As of 1999, about 12 percent of superintendents were women, and 5 to 10 percent of superintendents were nonwhite (Hodgkinson & Montenegro, 1999). With school boards it's not much better. According to the National School Boards Association, in 1997, 44 percent of all board members were women, but fewer than 10 percent were minority (National School Boards Association, 1999). This general lack of school board diversity will make it much more difficult for district organizations to be sensitive to cultural issues (Institute for Educational Leadership, 2001).

What America's superintendents do appear to agree on is that the profession is facing a crisis in attracting suitable candidates, thereby hastening the need to revamp the position to somehow increase its appeal and security (Cooper, et. al, 2000). What would improve the career situation? Most superintendents say a more attractive pay and benefit package would help recruit talented, new applicants to the superintendency (Fusarelli, et a., 2002). A very close second is getting additional help from the district (Cooper, et. al, 2000). Superintendents also agree that their careers are satisfying. Despite the fact that superintendents perceive a crisis in their profession, have concerns about the future recruitment of new applicants, and worry about job turnover (Cooper, et al., 2000), research shows that overall, they continue to be quite satisfied with their careers (Fusarelli, et al., 2002; Glass, 2000a; Glass, 2000d). They find their work challenging and rewarding, especially in building curriculum, assisting students, and contributing to society (Cooper, et al., 2000). Oddly, superintendents in large districts reported the highest career satisfaction (Fusarelli, et al., 2002). Yet while 91 percent "strongly agree" that their work provides "real career satisfaction," only 65 percent state they would recommend it as a "meaningful and satisfying career" (Cooper, et al., 2000). The AASA 10-year study in 2000 also showed that career satisfaction is high among superintendents, with 56 percent reporting "considerable fulfillment," and another 34 percent citing "moderate fulfillment." But, once more, only about two-thirds responded that they would choose the profession again as a career (Glass, 2000d).

The public's demand for education reform has had a significant impact on the traditional role of the superintendent (Owen & Ovando, 2000). The standards movement has shifted the superintendent further away from school district manager to that of testing expert (Glass, 2000c). National commission and task force reports published since the mid-1980s confirm that school and district administrators are vital to the effectiveness of school reform and call for improving the profession and changing the way superintendents of the next generation are identified, prepared, selected, and evaluated (Hoyle, et al., 2005). However, in a study of the 100 largest urban school districts in the United States, superintendents reported that the traditional training they received did not properly prepare them for the situations they face on the job, especially the politics of urban districts (Fuller, et al., 2003).

Management ability alone, while critically important, is no longer central to a superintendent's success. School systems can no longer survive long term with superintendents who have crafted their expertise only as good managers. Of course managing is still very important, but it has to be tempered with the ability of the superintendent to provide leadership on a number of fronts. Today managing exists to support and complement the educational leadership role and responsibility of the superintendent, since reforming school systems to conform with a new set of expectations requires a different focus. The superintendent's style and expertise must be heavily weighted toward educational leadership that promotes and reinforces innovative approaches to schooling. The superintendent/manager of past eras tended to be concerned with determining the goals to be accomplished and the best way to achieve tangible results. Educational leadership, however, is more concerned with accomplishing goals by breaking down traditional boundaries and involving more participants in defining problems, devising solutions, and mobilizing support for new initiatives that will improve student learning. This leadership style features the premise that the more people who are involved in the decision making process, the better the decision. Also at its root is the concept that the decisions made closest to where the action is are the best decisions.

These central themes have given rise to the new direction the superintendent/leader must take. Certainly shared decision making is not a new idea, but it is an idea that is viewed more seriously as the main focus has shifted to making a significant difference in student learning. It is generally accepted that school reform and similar movements to continuously improve the quality of education require a leader who reaches beyond employee control to establish a culture of empowerment within the organization (Dunn, 2001). The superintendents who are most productive will use their mastery of the profession and leadership skills to empower others to be change agents (Kowalski, 2001). It is up to the superintendent to assist the community in creating a system of schools that is in line with community values and beliefs, and one in which the community becomes a part of the school and the school becomes a part of the community (Owen & Ovando, 2000).

One specific program for site-based or school-centered education that has been successfully used in the Dallas, Texas school system incorporates the work of Yale University's James Comer and his School Development Program. It uses tailor-made plans and approaches to educate students, and transforms a traditional school system into exactly that, *a system of schools*. Obviously, the goal is to bring the entire school and community together to create a climate that encourages learning by placing autonomy and accountability where it counts: at the student level. As part of the program, each local school, along with that school's community, develops and implements a plan for improving student achievement, training staff members, and evaluating and modifying the program as it progresses.

While in this case the Dallas school board supported the plan, there may be initial resistance from board members when moving to a school-centered program. But it can be overcome. It helps to provide the board with in-depth research and information about the benefits, document everything that is done, make sure they understand the power structure, and of course, maintain open communications. With many different people and groups working toward the same goal, parents and community members at first weren't as confident that the program was anything new. They had to be convinced that they would have exciting roles under the school-centered program. Yet once parents and community members took part in the planning and decision making, district officials were actually overwhelmed with ideas and enthusiasm that resulted from the process (Edwards, 1993).

Along with meaningful school site involvement, decisions supported by data will take more of a center stage in the future. Data-driven decision making, like shared decision making, is not a new idea. Indeed, enlightened administrators have touted its power for years. However, in today's political climate, with the potential for a national curriculum, the idea of data-driven decisions has resurfaced with a renewed importance. Unlike the whispers of years past about how data could be used, it is becoming the buzzword of a larger number of school leaders. Administrators, including the superintendent, who do not know about or understand decision making supported by data will be left behind. In shared decision making, for example, school systems across the country, principals, and building level decision making committees use computers and databases to gather and dissect information about their schools.

Prior to the emphasis on data-driven shared decision making, one or two people—who were usually at the central office and understood data—would amass the statistics for the entire system. The information was then disseminated within the system to people who may or may not have understood the documents. In most cases, there was little or no training for the recipients on how to use the data in the reports. The problem with that model is that most of the staff, unfortunately including the leaders, were at the mercy of reports they had to accept but had no way to verify.

A big part of the success of the new data-driven movement is the training that precedes distributing information to the various users. With a better understanding of how to use the data, more decisions can be made that are supported by data. The superintendent who does not comprehend the power of data-driven, shared decision making will soon find himself or herself unable to communicate with an enlightened constituent base that comprehends what is behind good decisions.

A distinguishing characteristic of tomorrow's successful superintendent will be the ability to communicate effectively, which means a great deal more than communication in a traditional sense. Communicating effectively a few years ago meant that the superintendent was articulate and artful in the handling of language. It also meant that the superintendent was a good spokesperson for the district, with the ability to give speeches that held the attention of an audience interested in hearing about the school system. Today it means that and a great deal more. And it is the "great deal more" that can make the difference.

In earlier chapters, much attention was given to the superintendent's responsibility to seek out diverse interests in the school system and include them in district discussions. Moreover, strategic planning was highlighted as the mechanism for leading a school district through meaningful change. The new direction for leadership seems to point to more involvement on the part of all owners of the school system. The more diverse the participants are, the better the chances for the system to be successful or to improve.

Thus, an effective and broad-based communication system that creates a coalition of supporters for the improvements being made in the district will be behind the future superintendent's success (Carter & Cunningham, 1997). Without the leadership of a futuristic superintendent who understands the outcome of true collaboration, initiatives and changes will have little opportunity to succeed. The school board, after all, cannot as a corporate body make the kind of impact that one creative, forward-thinking superintendent can.

Another challenge that requires special effort is guiding the teachers' unions in becoming real partners in the educational enterprise instead of sideline pressure groups hoping to get a piece of the action. The old methods of doing business with unions need to be replaced with reasoned communication and involvement. The end result of the new pact has to be genuine trust and acceptance on both sides. Up until now, no matter how skilled the superintendent, the district's relationship with the unions was typically at arm's length, with the suspicion that the motive of the unions was to wrestle away power. The desired shift in attitude is difficult and will not occur merely because the superintendent wants it to. Nor will it happen through the desire of the school board. It must take place because union leaders also want the change, and are willing to take the risk that their members will still respect them if they become true allies of the system rather than the closet allies they were in the past. If both the administration and the unions do not embrace this forward-thinking mentality, the public will ultimately demand it in such a way that there will be little choice but to comply or become obsolete.

Shared decision making has many faces and requires regular contact to be successful. In the best models, decisions are made by groups. Members of these groups must talk with each other, and not just at meetings. In the future, it will not be unusual for school staff, including teachers, to be part of committees that make decisions at the district level. It has always been considered normal and expected that school staff would have an interest in the decision making process and participate at the site level. But the occasional appearance of school staff at district level activities sometimes produces apprehension. Under the old way of thinking and behaving, teachers and staff who volunteered to serve on citizens' committees were viewed with skepticism and suspicion. One standard of the past was that unions tended to assign members to serve on districtwide committees; teachers would not likely volunteer for such duty without the direction or blessings of union leadership. The loosening of the unions' grip is becoming evident as more and more teachers feel comfortable in volunteering to work on district level committees. The school board and the superintendent should not feel threatened by the presence of the rank and file teachers or staff. As previously mentioned, having so many diverse backgrounds around the table with voices that are valued will render most groups that seek to be disruptive ineffective. The charge to the unions is to approach these committees as full trusting partners or risk losing the respect of the larger body for not being willing to engage in meaningful change.

Some superintendents, on the other hand, may have trouble accepting all of this partnering and the implied erosion of their leadership. It is probably more a matter of personal confidence that will determine whether a superintendent can serve as the leader specified by the law as well as share power without giving away authority. It is a delicate balance to be sure, and will take a skilled superintendent to handle the responsibility. The superintendent in this future paradigm has to be an educational leader with all of the skills necessary to get the job done through investing the time and effort in building and maintaining alliances with people who will be empowered to assure the district's success (Dunn, 2001).

The superintendent's challenge is not to provide solutions, but facilitate a process through which dissonant voices, distinct interests, and conflicting viewpoints can work toward the best interest of the school system and the community (Carter & Cunningham, 1997). He or she must be the convener, and not the creator, of the educational agenda for the system. The fact that there are so many partners around the table with varied backgrounds only adds strength to the superintendent's leadership task. The best superintendents recognize that diverse backgrounds do not necessarily indicate conflicting interests around the question of improving the school system. Most constituents want the same things—they want a school system that works, and one that produces accomplished student learners, which is the same goal a good superintendent should have. This leadership model features many partners who unselfishly give of their time to support the superintendent's work. The lessons to be learned by building partnerships is that when the system is successful, the superintendent is successful. Even under this shared involvement model, when things go well, the superintendent will be praised as a great leader. And when things do not go well, the superintendent will ultimately be blamed.

To the extent that superintendents understand and acknowledge that the organizations they lead are not self-sufficient, they will exhibit their ability to serve as great educational leaders. The joint efforts of school districts and their communities are necessary for meaningful reform to occur (Kowalski, 2001). The interdependence that is becoming a standard for leadership excellence in this country has created both obligation and opportunity for superintendents. Twenty-first century superintendents are obligated to be the educational leaders of systems and not merely managers. This will require them to bring divergent interests from the entire school community together and demonstrate through action that these community members are valued for their contributions. Because of the desire to hear from as many different voices as possible, leaving any interest group out of the process will make the entire effort less effective. Paying attention to the various facets of communities and governments has allowed the unprecedented building of partnerships, as compared to any other time in our history. While interdependence as a leadership style limits the possibility of superintendents slipping back into the old top-down military model, it also expands the opportunity for collaboration and shared leadership between the school system and its community.

Both the skills required of superintendents and the environment in which they use those skills are changing. Superintendents need to spend much more of their time involved with community interests, accounting for state assessment mandates, and leading the charge for public education (Glass, 2000a). The key to success will depend on how responsive the superintendent is to the various demands (Carter & Cunningham, 1997). The superintendency today appears to be more closely linked than ever to forming cooperative working relationships with school boards and community groups. Excellence in communication, a full comprehension of the instructional process, and coalitions that ensure the financial and educational survival of the school district will be the mark of effective superintendents (Glass, 2000a). Thus, the school district's success ultimately resides with a courageous superintendent who is a proactive educational leader and considers the long-term consequences of how the system respects its community. It is through the superintendent's vision that a learning community which reflects the elements of a good school in the 21st century can be created—one that serves its students as well as everyone else interested in their education. That truly is a product of the modern school superintendency.

References

American Association of School Administrators-National School Boards Association Joint Committee. (1994). *Roles and relationships: School boards and superintendents* (Revised). Arlington, VA: The American Association of School Administrators.

Björk, L. (2000a). Personal characteristics. In T. Glass, L. Björk & C. Brunner (Eds.), *The study of the American school superintendency 2000: A look at the superintendent of education in the new millennium* (pp.15-32). Arlington, VA: American Association of School Administrators.

Björk, L. (2000b). Professional preparation and training. In T. Glass, L. Björk & C. Brunner (Eds.), *The study of the American school superintendency 2000: A look at the superintendent of education in the new millennium* (pp.127-161). Arlington, VA: American Association of School Administrators.

Björk, L. (2001). Institutional barriers to educational reform: A superintendent's role in district decentralization. In C. Brunner & L. Björk (Eds.), *The new superintendency. Advances in research and theories of school management and educational policy, vol. 6* (pp.205-228). Oxford, United Kingdom: JAI, an imprint of Elsevier Science.

Björk, L., & Keedy, J. (2001). Politics and the superintendency in the USA: Restructuring in-service education. *Journal of In-Service Education, vol. 27, no. 2*, 275-302.

Blumberg, A., with Blumberg, P. (1985). *The school superintendent: Living with conflict*. New York: Teachers College Press.

Brubacher, J. (1966). *A history of the problems of education.* (2nd ed.). New York: McGraw-Hill.

Brunner, C., & Björk, L. (Eds.). (2001). *The new superintendency. Advances in research and theories of school management and educational policy, vol. 6.* Oxford, United Kingdom: JAI, an imprint of Elsevier Science.

Butts, R., & Cremin, L. (1953). *A history of education in American culture.* New York: Henry Holt & Co.

Callahan, R. (1966). *The superintendent of schools: A historical analysis.* ERIC Document Reproduction Service No. ED 0104 410.

Cambron-McCabe, N., Cunningham, L., Harvey, J., & Koff, R. (2005). *The superintendent's fieldbook: A guide for leaders of learning.* Thousand Oaks, CA: A joint publication of the American Association of School Administrators and Corwin Press.

Cambron-McCabe, N., & Harvey, J. (2005). Leading your schools: Thinking about your organization—Images of organization. In N. Cambron-McCabe, L. Cunningham, J. Harvey & R. Koff, *The superintendent's fieldbook: A guide for leaders of learning* (pp.19-30). Thousand Oaks, CA: A joint publication of the American Association of School Superintendents and Corwin Press.

Campbell, R., Cunningham, L., Nystrand, R., & Usdan, M. (1990). *The organization and control of American schools* (6th ed.). Upper Saddle, NJ: Merrill/Prentice Hall.

Carter, G., & Cunningham, W. (1997). *The American school superintendent: Leading in an age of pressure.* San Francisco: Jossey-Bass.

Chapman, C. (1997). *Becoming a superintendent: Challenges of school district leadership.* Upper Saddle, NJ: Merrill/Prentice Hall.

Chapman, C., & Chapman, S. (1997). Harsh realities: Politics, corruption, and immorality. In C. Chapman, *Becoming a superintendent: Challenges of school district leadership* (pp.209-218). Upper Saddle, NJ: Merrill/Prentice Hall.

Cooper, B., & Fusarelli, L. (Eds.). (2002). *The promises and perils facing today's school superintendent.* Lanham, MD: The Scarecrow Press.

Cooper, B., Fusarelli, L., & Carella, V. (2000). *Career crisis in the superintendency? The results of a national survey.* Arlington, VA: American Association of School Administrators.

Cunningham, L., & Hentges, J. (1982). *The American school superintendency 1982: A summary report.* Arlington, VA: American Association of School Administrators.

Danzberger, J. (1998). School boards—Partners in policy. In R. Spillane & P. Regnier, *The superintendent of the future: Strategy and action for achieving academic excellence* (pp.191-218). Gaithersburg, MD: Aspen Publishers.

Darling-Hammond, L. (2004). In D. Meier & G. Wood (Eds.), *Many children left behind: How the no child left behind act is damaging our children and our schools* (pp.3-32). Boston: Beacon Press.

Dunn, R. (2001). Community and control in the superintendency. In C. Brunner & L. Björk (Eds.), *The new superintendency: Advances in research and theories of school management and educational policy, vol. 6* (pp.153-168). Oxford, United Kingdom: JAI, an imprint of Elsevier Science.

Eadie, D. (2003). *Eight keys to an extraordinary board-superintendent partnership.* Lanham, MD: The Scarecrow Press.

Education Commission of the States. (2005, March). *What's happening in school and district leadership?* Denver, CO: Education Commission of the States.

Edwards, M. (1993, May). Restructuring in Dallas—The school-based management plan in this urban district creates a climate that helps children achieve. *The American School Board Journal*, 30-32.

Estes, N. (2002). Director of the Cooperative Superintendency Program at The University of Texas at Austin, College of Education. [Telephone interview with the author.]

Farkas, S., Johnson, J., & Duffett, A., with Syat, B., & Vine, J. (2003). *Rolling up their sleeves: Superintendents and principals talk about what's needed to fix schools*. Public Agenda Online: Public Agenda with The Wallace Foundation. [Online]. Retrieved from http://www.publicagenda.org/specials/rollingup/rollingup.htm.

Forman, G. (1998). Nuts and bolts. In R. Spillane & P. Regnier, *The superintendent of the future: Strategy and action for achieving academic excellence* (pp.117-156). Gaithersburg, MD: Aspen Publishers.

Fuller, H., with Campbell, C., Cello, M., Harvey, J., Immerwahr, J., & Winger, A. (2003, July). *An impossible job? The view from the urban superintendent's chair*. Seattle, WA: Center on Reinventing Public Education.

Fuller, H., & Harvey, J. (2005). Addressing race and class: Orientation: Why race and class? In N. Cambron-McCabe, L. Cunningham, J. Harvey & R. Koff, *The superintendent's fieldbook: A guide for leaders of learning* (pp.143-146). Thousand Oaks, CA: A joint publication of the American Association of School Superintendents and Corwin Press.

Fusarelli, L., Cooper, B., & Carella, V. (2002). Dilemmas of the modern superintendency. In B. Cooper & L. Fusarelli (Eds.), *The promises and perils facing today's school superintendent* (pp. 5-20). Lanham, MD: The Scarecrow Press.

Glasman, N., & Fuller, J. (2002). Superintendent evaluation: Concepts, practices, and an outcome-related case. In B. Cooper & L. Fusarelli

(Eds.), *The promises and perils facing today's school superintendent* (pp.139-152). Lanham, MD: The Scarecrow Press.

Glass, T. (1992). *The 1992 study of the American school superintendency: America's education leaders in a time of reform*. Arlington, VA: American Association of School Administrators.

Glass, T. (1997). The superintendency: Yesterday, today, and tomorrow. In C. Chapman, *Becoming a superintendent: Challenges of school district leadership* (pp.19-39). Upper Saddle, NJ: Merrill/Prentice Hall.

Glass, T. (2000a). Executive Summary. In T. Glass, L. Björk & C. Brunner (Eds.), *The study of the American school superintendency 2000: A look at the superintendent of education in the new millennium* (pp. iii-x). Arlington, VA: American Association of School Administrators.

Glass, T. (2000b). Professional experience. In T. Glass, L. Björk & C. Brunner (Eds.), *The study of the American school superintendency 2000: A look at the superintendent of education in the new millennium* (pp. 33-52). Arlington, VA: American Association of School Administrators.

Glass, T. (2000c). The superintendency. In T. Glass, L. Björk & C. Brunner (Eds.), *The study of the American school superintendency 2000: A look at the superintendent of education in the new millennium* (pp.1-8). Arlington, VA: American Association of School Administrators.

Glass, T. (2000d). Superintendent/school board relations. In T. Glass, L. Björk & C. Brunner (Eds.), *The study of the American school superintendency 2000: A look at the superintendent of education in the new millennium* (pp.53-76). Arlington, VA: American Association of School Administrators.

Glass, T., Björk, L., & Brunner, C. (2000). *The study of the American school superintendency 2000: A look at the superintendent of education in the new millennium*. Arlington, VA: American Association of School Administrators.

Harvey, J. (2005a). Addressing case and class: Orientation: Why race and class? In N. Cambron-McCabe, L. Cunningham, J. Harvey & R. Koff, *The superintendent's fieldbook: A guide for leaders of learning* (pp.143-146). Thousand Oaks, CA: A joint publication of the American Association of School Superintendents and Corwin Press.

Harvey, J. (2005b). Collaborating with your allies: What does collaboration require? Build boats, not houses. In N. Cambron-McCabe, L. Cunningham, J. Harvey & R. Koff, *The superintendent's fieldbook: A guide for leaders of learning* (pp.229-231). Thousand Oaks, CA: A joint publication of the American Association of School Superintendents and Corwin Press.

Harvey, J. (2005c). Understanding standards and assessment: Orientation—The shape of the new discussion. In N. Cambron-McCabe, L. Cunningham, J. Harvey & R. Koff, *The superintendent's fieldbook: A guide for leaders of learning* (pp.109-113). Thousand Oaks, CA: A joint publication of the American Association of School Superintendents and Corwin Press.

Harvey, J., & Wallace, R., Jr. (2005). Understanding standards and assessment: Orientation—No child left behind and adequate yearly progress. In N. Cambron-McCabe, L. Cunningham, J. Harvey & R. Koff, *The superintendent's fieldbook: A guide for leaders of learning* (pp. 113-114). Thousand Oaks, CA: A joint publication of the American Association of School Superintendents and Corwin Press.

Hayes, W. (2001). *So you want to be a superintendent?* Lanham, MD: The Scarecrow Press.

Hodgkinson, H., & Montenegro, X. (1999). *The U.S. school superintendent: The invisible CEO.* Washington, D.C.: Institute for Eductaional Leadership.

Houston, P. (1997). Forward. In G. Carter & W. Cunningham, *The American school superintendent: Leading in an age of pressure* (pp. xi-xv). San Francisco: Jossey-Bass.

Houston, P., & Eadie, D. (2002). The board-savvy superintendent. Lanham, MD: The Scarecrow Press.

Hoyle, J. (1993). *Professional standards for the superintendency*. Arlington, VA: American Association of School Administrators.

Hoyle, J., Björk, L., Collier, V., & Glass, T. (2005). *The superintendent as CEO: Standards-based performance*. Thousand Oaks, CA: Corwin Press.

Hoyle, J., English, F., & Steffy, B. (1998). *Skills for successful 21st century school leaders: Standards for peak performers*. Arlington, VA: American Association of School Administrators.

Institute for Educational Leadership. (2001, February). *Leadership for student learning: Restructuring school district leadership school leadership. School leadership for the 21st century initiative. A report of the task force on school district leadership*. Washington, D.C.: Institute for Educational Leadership.

Johnson, S. (1996). *Leading to change: The challenge of the new superintendency*. San Francisco: Jossey-Bass.

Kowalski, T. (1999). *The school superintendent: Theory, practice and cases*. Saddle River, NJ: Merrill/Prentice-Hall.

Kowalski, T. (2001). The future of local school governance: Implications for board members and superintendents. In C. Brunner & L. Björk (Eds.), *The new superintendency: Advances in research and theories of school management and educational policy, vol. 6* (pp.183-201). Oxford, United Kingdom: JAI, an imprint of Elsevier Science.

Kowalski, T., & Glass, T. (2002). Preparing superintendents for the 21st century. In B. Cooper & L. Fusarelli (Eds.), *The promises and perils facing today's school superintendent* (pp. 41-59). Lanham, MD: The Scarecrow Press.

National Commission on Excellence in Educational Administration. (1987). *Leaders for America's schools.* Tempe, AZ: University Council of Educational Administration.

National Policy Board for Educational Administration. (1989, May). *Improving the preparation of school administrators: An agenda for reform.* Charlottesville, VA: The National Policy Board for Educational Administration.

National School Boards Association. (1999). *Educational vital signs 1999.* Alexandria, VA: National School Boards Association. [Online]. Retrieved from http://www.asbj.com/evs/99/index.html.

Norton, M., Webb, L., Dlugosh, L., & Sybouts, W. (1996). *The school superintendency: New responsibilities, new leadership.* Needham Heights, MA: Allyn and Bacon.

Owen, J., & Ovando, M. (2000). *Superintendents's guide to creating community.* Lanham, MD: The Scarecrow Press.

Pendleton, B., & Benjamin, R. (2005). Engaging your community: Orientation. In N. Cambron-McCabe, L. Cunningham, J. Harvey & R. Koff, *The superintendent's fieldbook: A guide for leaders of learning* (pp. 259-260). Thousand Oaks, CA: A joint publication of the American Association of School Superintendents and Corwin Press.

Peterkin, R. (2002). Director of the Concentration in the Urban Superintendency in the Urban Superintendents Program at Harvard University, Harvard Graduate School of Education. [Telephone interview with the author.]

Popham, W. (2004). *America's "failing" schools: How parents and teachers can cope with no child left behind*. New York: RoutledgeFalmer.

Public Agenda Online. (2001, Special ed.). *Trying to stay ahead of the game: Superintendents and principals talk about school leadership*. [Online]. Retrieved from http://www.publicagenda.org/specials/leadership/leadership.htm.

Ramsey, R. (1999). *Lead, follow, or get out of the way: How to be a more effective leader in today's schools*. Thousand Oaks, CA: Corwin Press.

Scott, H. (1980). *The black school superintendent: Messiah or scapegoat?* Washington, D.C.: Howard University Press.

Sharp, W., & Sharp, H. (2004). Appendix C: Site-based management: A practical guide. In W. Sharp & J. Walter, *The school superintendent: The profession and the person* (2nd ed., pp. 247-251). Lanham, MD: Scarecrow Press.

Sharp, W., & Walter, J. (2004). *The school superintendent: The profession and the person* (2nd ed.). Lanham, MD: Scarecrow Press.

Shibles, M., Rallis, S., & Deck, L. (2001). A new political balance between superintendent and board: Clarifying purpose and generating knowledge. In C. Brunner & L. Björk (Eds.), *The new superintendency. Advances in research and theories of school management and educational policy, vol. 6* (pp.169-181). Oxford, United Kingdom: JAI, an imprint of Elsevier Science.

Spring, J. (1998). *Conflict of interests: The politics of American education* (3rd ed.). Boston: McGraw-Hill.

Tallerico, M. (2000). *Accessing the superintendency: The unwritten rules*. Thousand Oaks, CA: A joint publication of the American Association of School Administrators and Corwin Press.

Townsend, R., Brown, J., & Buster, W. (2005). *A practical guide to effective school board meetings.* Thousand Oaks, CA: Corwin Press.

Wallace, R., Jr. (2005). Coping with governance challenges: Working with your board—School finance 101: No surprise around money. In N. Cambron-McCabe, L. Cunningham, J. Harvey & R. Koff, *The superintendent's fieldbook: A guide for leaders of learning* (pp. 89-90). Thousand Oaks, CA: A joint publication of the American Association of School Superintendents and Corwin Press.

Weiss, C. (1993, February). Interests and ideologies in educational reform: Changing the venue of decision making in high school (Occasional paper no. 19). Cambridge, MA: National Center for Educational Leadership.

Wood, G. (2004). Introduction. In D. Meier & G. Wood (Eds.), *Many children left behind: How the no child left behind act is damaging our children and our schools* (pp. vii-xv). Boston: Beacon Press.

About the Author

Marvin E. Edwards is the director of the Center for Educational Executives at Aurora University in Aurora, Illinois. He also serves as an associate professor for educational leadership in the doctoral program, with his research emphasis on the school superintendent.

Edwards earned his Bachelor of Science degree (1967) in education at Eastern Illinois University, Charleston; his Master of Science degree (1970) at Chicago State University; his Certificate of Advanced Study degree (1973) at Northern Illinois University, DeKalb; and his Educational Doctorate degree (1974) in educational leadership at Northern Illinois University.

During his 35 years in public education, Edwards has enjoyed a distinguished career as a teacher and school leader. High school principal, dean of students, department chair, and assistant superintendent are among the variety of administrative posts he has held prior to becoming a superintendent. His 23 years as a superintendent have included the top position in Dallas, Texas; Topeka, Kansas; and Joliet, Illinois. Edwards has also been an adjunct professor at several colleges and universities. After serving nine years as superintendent of schools in Elgin, Illinois—the state's second largest school district—Edwards joined Aurora University.

In 1998, Edwards was selected as the Illinois Superintendent of the Year and was recognized as one of four top school superintendents in the nation. The following year, the Illinois chapter of the National School Public Relations Association honored him with its annual award for his distinguished work as a superintendent. In 2000, the National School Public Relations Association honored Edwards with the prestigious Bob Grossman Leadership in School Communications Award—its highest honor—which is given annually to a practicing school superintendent or CEO of an education agency, service center or intermediary unit for outstanding school public relations and communications leadership.

Innovations have marked Edwards's career as an education leader. He is noted for implementing reform initiatives such as: the School-Centered Education program in Dallas, where a unique form of site-based management held principals and faculty accountable for improved student achievement; enhanced early childhood education programs in Elgin, along with year-round schools and gifted academies; and formal leadership training for aspiring administrators.

Edwards has published articles on school reform, school and community relations, leadership, and school accountability. But his main focus has been on leadership, and the superintendency in particular. Through his work at Aurora University and as an independent consultant, Edwards has advised many school boards on their selection of a superintendent, as well as counseled aspiring superintendents in their quest to obtain a superintendency.

978-0-595-40874-0
0-595-40874-5

Printed in the United States
87806LV00004B/139/A